Manual for
Theory and Practice
of Group Counseling

Manual for
Theory and Practice
of Group Counseling

Gerald Corey

California State University, Fullerton

Brooks/Cole Publishing Company
Monterey, California

Brooks/Cole Publishing Company
A Division of Wadsworth, Inc.

Printed in the United States of America

10 9 8 7 6 5 4 3 2

BF637.C6C576   616.89'152   80-18985

ISBN: 0-8185-0432-3

Acquisition Editor: Claire Verduin
Production Editor: Stacey C. Sawyer
Cover Design: Charles Carter
Typewriter Composition: Betty Ritter

To my students in the <u>Practicum in Group Leadership</u>
classes at California State University at Fullerton,
who helped in refining the ideas and exercises in
the manual.

Acknowledgments

I wish to thank my students at California State University at Fullerton, who used the material in this manual in the Practicum in Group Leadership course. They provided helpful suggestions by indicating which exercises were most valuable and naming the parts that were least useful.

Let me give special recognition to several students who served as reviewers of the manual in its developmental stages: Randy Corliss, Donna Robbins, Diane Vasquez, and Merri Chalenor. They made many valuable suggestions, which I think have enhanced the student appeal of this manual. Robert Cash of California State University at Long Beach also reviewed the manuscript.

Special thanks go to my wife (and colleague and friend) who helped devise many of the exercises and activities as we sat on our balcony in Idyllwild. I also am indebted to my close friends and colleagues for inspiration and challenge in developing the material in the manual. They are Patrick Callanan and J. Michael Russell of California State University at Fullerton.

I invite you to express your ideas and your reactions to both this manual and the textbook, Theory and Practice of Group Counseling, by writing me at Brooks/Cole Publishing Company, Monterey, California, 93940. I look forward to receiving your ideas on how to make the text and the manual more useful.

Gerald Corey

Contents

PART
I

Basic Elements
of Group Process:
An Overview

CHAPTER

1

Introduction

This manual is designed to accompany <u>Theory and Practice of Group Counseling</u> by Gerald Corey (Brooks/Cole, 1981). The purpose of the manual is to assist you in gaining some practical experience in working with the concepts and techniques of the various theoretical approaches to group work, as well as stimulating thought on basic ethical and professional issues typically encountered by group leaders.

I hope the material in this manual will aid your own personal growth. Much of this material consists of things you can think about, experiment with, and do on your own; and much of the material consists of exercises that you can practice in small groups, both as a leader and as a member. You'll be provided with opportunities to function in numerous role-playing situations, which can be very real and very instructive. I encourage you to modify these exercises so that they will become personally meaningful.

The design of the manual is based on the assumption that you will learn about the practical applications of group techniques by becoming actively involved in the learning process and by <u>actually experiencing</u> these concepts and techniques. Reading about them provides a foundation, yet this knowledge remains abstract unless students can see how these theories actually work in groups.

Some of the exercise material includes:

a. self-inventories to assess your attitudes about various theories;

b. open-ended questions for discussion and evaluation;

c. ideas and suggestions for role playing;

d. techniques for group interaction;

e. practical problems that occur in groups;

f. group exercises for experiential practice; and

g. suggestions of things you can do to apply what you are learning in the course to yourself personally and to yourself as a group leader.

There is more material in this manual than a given course can thoroughly cover. However, my preference is to provide a wide variety of questions and activities so that you can select the ones that you find most meaningful. The questions in this manual give a focus to your reading and will help you read and study in an active way.

HOW TO USE THE MANUAL AND THE TEXTBOOK

Below are some suggestions for getting the maximum value from the text-book and the manual. These suggestions are based on my experience in teaching this course and using the material in classes. My students have found the following guidelines to be of help in integrating and applying what they are studying.

1. First, I recommend looking over all the contents of the manual to get an overview of the course and the reading program.

2. Before you read and study a chapter in the textbook, read any summary material in the corresponding chapter in the manual, and look over the "Questions for Discussion and Evaluation," if they are included in that chapter. For the chapters that deal with theories of group counseling (Part Two), complete the manual's corresponding prechapter primer and self-inventory, which is based on the key concepts dis-cussed in the textbook. Completing these self-inventories will help you to determine the degree to which you agree or disagree with the concepts of a given theory. Taking these inventories and spending a few minutes reviewing them will give you a clearer focus on the chapter you're reading in the textbook.

3. After reading and studying a chapter in the textbook, return to the manual to:

   a. review any questions for discussion, select the questions that will help you best put the theory or issues into focus, and for-mulate your own positions on these questions;

   b. if you have just finished a chapter on theory, retake or at least review the prechapter primer to see if your views have changed;

   c. for theoretical chapters, study the summary/overview charts that describe in brief form the developmental stages of a group, ac-cording to the particular theory;

   d. look over the basic assumptions and summary of key concepts of the theory;

   e. select some exercises to do on your own and some to do in a group.

4. Perhaps most important, get some actual experience in working in small classroom groups with the concepts and techniques of the vari-ous counseling approaches. The more you are willing to invest your-self in an active manner in small group work, the more you'll be able to see the possibilities for actually using these techniques in groups you lead. Again, I have provided more small-group activities

than can be done in even a two-hour self-directed group for training purposes. It is not expected that you do all these exercises; your group should select several of them and experiment with them.

In my course, in addition to the weekly seminars and class meetings where we discuss the theory of group work, the students also meet in small experiential groups for up to two hours a week to gain practice in being a group member and in taking turns coleading a group. Each week they work within the framework of the model we are studying in class, and in this way they get a better idea of how therapies are actually applied in a group. The students experience the problems involved in making the translation from theory to practice, they find out what aspects of each theory they want to incorporate into their style of group leadership, and they learn by interacting with their peers.

You are encouraged to use your ingenuity with the exercises that are presented. Use them as a springboard for developing your own exercises. Think of different ways that you might use the techniques you learn in the groups you lead.

5. Theory and Practice of Group Counseling is designed as a survey textbook, and, as such, it can't provide an advanced and detailed treatment of the theories presented. My aim has been to introduce you to some of the key concepts of a variety of theories underlying group practice and to describe some of the therapeutic techniques that flow from these concepts. I hope that when you finish studying the textbook and manual you will want to read more about some of the therapies. Following each chapter on theory is an annotated list of recommended supplementary reading that will give you additional information.

6. The manual is designed as a guide and a resource to help you eventually create your own theory and style of group leading. Toward this end, I recommend that, as you read and study the chapters in both the textbook and the manual, you look for both the characteristics shared by the approaches and the major differences among them, determine the unique characteristics of each model, and select specific aspects of each approach that appear to be suited to your personality. The manual's main purpose is to make these theories and issues come alive to you. To accomplish this it is essential that you involve yourself actively by thinking critically, share your thoughts with others in class, and invest yourself emotionally by bringing your own life experiences into this program.

2

Stages in the Development of a Group

EXERCISES AND ACTIVITIES

As a group leader, your knowledge of the stages in the development of a group can help you carry out specific functions at these various phases. By being aware of the characteristics of groups at different stages in their evolution, you can provide needed structure, make appropriate interventions, and predict certain blocks to group process. These exercises and activities will give you practice in your class or groups in developing the leadership skills needed at each stage. As you read through these activities, select the ones that have the most meaning for you and bring them up in class/group. You can use some of them on your own as a way of learning techniques for organizing groups, establishing and maintaining a working climate, terminating groups, and opening or closing group sessions.

1. Developing a proposal. One of the first steps in organizing a group is writing a proposal. There are many kinds of questions that you might want to address in your proposal, including: What type of group will it be? For whom? For what purpose? How will you achieve your goals? What kind of selection process will be used? What format will the group follow? Will you have a topical orientation? What kind of evaluation will be used? Any follow-up devices?

    Think of additional questions to answer in your proposal so that whoever reads it will have a clear idea of what your group is about.

2. In your class/group you could try this experiment. Set up a situation where your fellow students can assume the role of colleagues in a counseling agency. Assume that you have a group that you'd like to get started at the agency. Present your proposal to your colleagues verbally; invite questions from them, as well as a response to your group proposal. Ask them if they would support your ideas for your program. Why or why not?

3. Imagine talking to potential group members. Explain to them what your group is for and how you expect to lead it. Assume that these people have never been in a group before. What would you stress regarding its purposes and procedures?

4. Screening-interview exercise. Assume the role of a group leader conducting a screening interview for members of a certain kind of group. Conduct a pregroup interview with a prospective member for about ten minutes. After the interview, the one who was interviewed can report on how he or she felt during the interview. What is your interviewing style like? What were some of the most effective questions or interventions? How could the interview have been improved? Then, interview another prospective member so that you can gain from the feedback and try new ideas.

5. Group member interviews the leader. Prospective members may want to talk with the leader before they commit themselves to a group. In this exercise, the same format can be used as in Exercise 4 except the group member (several people in class can volunteer for this role) asks questions of the group leader. This exercise can be done in subgroups so that everyone has a chance to be both the group member and the group leader. Everyone can be invited to make observations and suggestions.

6. Draw up a list of specific questions you might ask at a screening interview. What would you look for? On what basis would you include and exclude members?

7. How would you turn away a person if you thought that either he or she was not appropriate for the group or the group was not appropriate for him or her? You might set this up as a group/class exercise. Are you able not to accept a person in a group without conveying rejection?

8. What screening methods, if any, could you apply to an involuntary population? Do you believe that people who are involuntarily in a group can benefit from it? Why or why not? How would you deal with the situation if the agency you worked for insisted that all of the clients attended group, whether they wanted to or not? Assume that all the mental-health workers there had to use group therapy as the primary treatment method.

9. What would be your rationale for deciding on a homogeneous or a heterogeneous group? Discuss your reasons for your preference. What characteristics would you want group members to have in common?

10. Discuss some of the problems that you might encounter in an open group that you would not be as likely to have in a closed group. How do you expect to deal with the problems that arise in an open group (one with changing membership)?

11. What value, if any, do you see in arranging an initial private interview with each group member to explore matters such as goals, fears, expectations, questions, and concerns? How would you prepare members of your group?

12. Initial stages of a group. Try to recall what it was like for you when you first entered a counseling group or any group of strangers. Consider

the possibility that your prospective group members feel the same way. Discuss with others in your class/group how you might be a more compassionate leader if you could keep these memories fresh.

13. <u>Initial-session exercise</u>. To give you practice in opening a new group, form subgroups of about eight people. Two of you can volunteer to be coleaders, and the rest are members. The coleaders' task is to give a brief orientation. Consider some of the following ideas as a way of orienting your group:

   a. Give about a 15-minute <u>preparation talk</u> to group members. Tell them the things you'd <u>most</u> want them to know so that they'll function more effectively as participants throughout the course of the group.

   b. Consider discussing the purpose of the group, the nature of the group as you see it, any ground rules, and any other pertinent information.

   c. Think about telling the members something about yourself. Why are you leading groups? How do you get yourself ready for each group session?

   The members can be given the opportunity to ask questions or to talk about their expectations. After about a half hour or so, discuss the exercise. Members can share how they felt during the session, and constructive feedback can be given to the coleaders.

14. <u>Trust building</u>. What do you think are the most crucial tasks during the early stages of a group? Think of the ways that, as a group leader, you would attempt to create trust within the group. Also, think about ways you would introduce yourself to your group and how you'd take care of introductions of group members. What are some specific ways you might work on building trust at the initial meetings?

15. What are some possible explanations for the negative feelings and conflict that typically occur in a group's initial developmental stages— before members feel free enough to experience positive feelings?

16. Most writers describe conflict, confrontations, competition, rivalry, and jockeying for power as a basic part of a group's evolution. What could you do as a leader to ignore these dynamics? What effect would this have on subsequent group development?

17. Assume that you are leading your first group, and several members are questioning your level of expertise. How would you deal with this?

18. Imagine you are a group leader and the group members are challenging you by telling you that they see you strictly as "the leader." They ask you to become more like they are and share more of yourself with them. How would you handle this situation? Explain to the group your understanding of the role of group leader.

19. <u>Cohesion</u> is a key precondition for effective group work. To what degree do you agree or disagree with this view? What factors do you think are

7

specifically related to cohesion? What criterion would you use to determine the degree of cohesion? What can you think of doing with a group that would not develop a sense of unity?

20. Refer, in the textbook, to the characteristics of the effective and working group. What factors do you think are most significant? Discuss your reasons.

HELPFUL INTERVENTION PHRASES FOR THE INITIAL STAGE OF A GROUP

A few well-chosen words that are timed well can give group members the guidance that will enable them to explore personal issues in a significant way. Based on my own work with groups and my training of and consultation with group leaders, I have compiled a list of sentences and phrases that leaders can use during the beginning stage of a group. It might be helpful for you to review the list frequently before you begin a group, almost like using a checklist.

• Are you here because you want to be?

• What do you most want to get from this group?

• What are you willing to do to get what you say you want?

• Are you willing to try out new things in here?

• What are three things you want us to know about you?

• If you were to introduce yourself as the person you'd like to be, what would you tell us about you?

• What do you know about groups? With what expectations are you coming to this group?

• If a friend of yours were to introduce you to this group, what might he or she say about you?

• What was going on in your life that led you to join this group?

• What is it like for you to be here now?

• What fears or doubts do you have about this group, if any?

• What do you imagine would happen if you were to say the most difficult thing?

• What do you fear most? What do you hope for most?

• Why would you want to change anything in your life now?

• What would you most like to say you've learned or decided when you leave group?

- Realize that you'll take from this group what you are willing to put into it.

- If you are feeling something in here persistently, express it.

- How do you usually introduce yourself? What do you tell people about yourself?

HELPFUL INTERVENTION PHRASES FOR
THE WORKING STAGES OF A GROUP

The following are some sentences and phrases that you might find helpful once your group gets under way and people are working. Again, these are not merely clichés, rather they are specific statements that can serve as constructive interventions <u>if</u> you use them in context with a sense for timing. For example, if you sense that a member is leaving something out, you might intervene with "What are you not saying that needs to be said now?" If these brief interventions are done appropriately, members can be given a gentle impetus to continue. As you lead groups, think of the phrases that are useful to you. Below are some that my coleaders and I use.

- This silence doesn't feel good to me.

- I've noticed that you have been very quiet during this session, and I'd like to know how you feel.

- What would you like to do?

- Have any of you had any thoughts about our last session that you'd like to share?

- What else needs to be said?

- How were you affected by _____?

- How does this issue relate to you?

- Are you willing to continue now?

- I'd like each person in the group to finish the sentence "_____
. . ."

- Imagine this is the last chance you have to change your life.

- I'd like you to hold on to this feeling for a little longer.

- Could we have everyone say what he or she is feeling or thinking right now?

- I'd like to check out with the group how each of you experiences the energy level in the room.

- I like it when you _____.

- Right now I am aware of _____.

- Would you be willing to try this experiment to see how it works for you?

- What is your objection to continuing?

- Are you willing to explore the reasons for your reluctance to pursue this topic further?

- Whom do you have unfinished business with in here?

- What do you want to be able to say about yourself at our last session?

- Are you expecting change to be easy?

- How are each of you doing with your homework outside of the group?

- If this were to be the end of the group, would that be alright?

- Imagine that the significant person were here now. What would you want to say to her?

- Don't ask him questions. Tell him how it is for you.

- Are you willing to convert your question into a statement?

- What's the worst thing that you can imagine would happen if you continue now?

- If you never change in this respect, would that be so bad?

- I notice that _____.

- I'm interested in _____.

- I hope you'll consider _____.

- My hunch is _____.

- If your eyes could speak now, what would they say?

- What are you willing to do with the tension you feel?

- What will help you to remember what is being said to you?

- You experienced a lot of emotions during this session. What did you learn about yourself from this?

- What decision did you make about yourself in that situation when you were a child?

- You may have told yourself as a child that you had to be that way to survive, but now that decision doesn't seem appropriate.

- Become each part of your dream. Give each part a voice.

- Be that child now.

- Instead of talking about this situation, I'd like you to live it as though it were happening now.

- If your mother were here, what would you say to her now that you didn't tell her then?

- I'm aware of a good bit of resistance and holding back with many of you here, and I'd like to explore this.

- You have continued indoctrinating yourself with propaganda that you got from your parents. What new sentences could you begin to tell yourself?

- Instead of saying "I can't," say, "I won't."

- What can you do between this session and the next to practice what you've just learned?

- I'm feeling as though I'm working too hard at leading; almost as though I'm pulling teeth. I'd like to check out how others are feeling about this.

- I think it's important that each of you ask if you are getting what you want from this group and if there are any changes you'd like to see.

- So, some of you say you are bored. What are you going to do about this boredom?

- I'd like to review our contracts to determine if any of them need to be revised or updated.

HELPFUL INTERVENTION PHRASES FOR
THE ENDING STAGES OF A GROUP

During the consolidation stage of a group it is important for members to think of ways to apply what they've learned in the group to everyday life, to be able to take care of unfinished business, to be able to express their feelings regarding separation, and to make sense of the total group experience. Some of the following phrases and sentences are ones that I frequently use during the ending stages of a group. As you review this list, think of additional statements and questions that would help members accomplish the tasks at this stage of the group.

- What has this group meant to you?

- What are some of the most important things you learned about yourself?

- Are there any things you want to say to anyone in here?

- How do you feel about saying good-bye?

- I'm aware of the tendency to forget what we learn in group, so I'd like to talk about ways that you can remember what you did learn.

- How can you practice what you learned in here?

- How do you think you'll be different? Don't tell them, show them!

- Whom do you need to talk with outside of the group? What is the essence of what you want them to hear?

- What decisions have you made?

- If we were to meet one year from now as a group, what would you want to say that you've accomplished?

- If you had to say your message in <u>one sentence</u>, what would it be?

- Where can you go from here, now that the group is ending?

- How might you discount what you've learned in here?

- How can you translate insight into action?

- I hope each of you will find at least one person in this group to contact if you discover that you aren't putting your plans into action.

- I'd like to spend some time exploring where each of you can go from here, now that our group is ending.

- Let's practice and role-play some of the situations that each of you expects to encounter after you leave the group.

- To what degree did you attain your goals?

CHAPTER

3

Group Membership

EXERCISES AND ACTIVITIES

These exercises and activities will give you, as a group leader, some experience in working with the wide range of people that you may encounter in your group. Do as many of these activities as you can in small groups where you can alternately play the roles of group member and group leader. Again, select the exercises that seem most meaningful to you and take the initiative to bring them up in your group/class. Think of additional activities to give you practice in being both leader and member.

1. Refer to the section in the textbook on preparation of group members. In order to get the most from the group, what would you stress to the members? During the early stages of the group, what would you teach the members about group process?

2. Draw up your own list of "rights of group members." What do you think members have a right to know before they join a group? Once they are in a group, what are their most important rights? Add to this list what you consider their responsibilities to be as group participants. Check your list against some of the rights of group members described in the textbook.

3. Draw up a list of the skills you consider to be most necessary for effective group participation.

4. As a group leader, <u>how</u> would you go about teaching group members certain attitudes and behaviors, such as attending and responding, empathy, respect, concreteness, self-disclosure, and confrontation?

5. What is self-disclosure? What is it not? What is the purpose of group-member self-disclosure? What are some specific guidelines that are useful in teaching participants the skills involved in appropriate self-disclosure?

6. What is the purpose of confrontation? How can it be done by members in a constructive way? What would you tell members concerning the manner of confronting?

7. What are your ideas concerning resistance? Do you see resistance as an inevitable part of group process, or can it be avoided through skillful leadership?

8. Read the section in the textbook on resistance and forms of avoidance behavior in group members. Examine your own patterns of resistance as a group member. List some ways that you've found yourself resistant in this class/group. How many of the resistant and problem behaviors that are described in the text have you recognized in yourself? Imagine that you are leading a group of people that have many of the same defenses and resistances that you have. How would this be for you?

9. In your own experience as a group member, what has helped you to recognize and to work through certain resistances?. What has hindered you? What might have led you to deeper entrenchment into certain resistances and defensive styles of behaving in group?

10. Can you respect resistance? Assume that a member says that she doesn't want to press onward with an issue she's been working on. What course of action would you be inclined to take? Do you see a difference between pressuring members to talk about a given issue and encouraging them to talk about possible fears that keep them from working on the issue?

11. What can a group leader do in general to effectively handle resistances that occur in a group? What are helpful leader behaviors in a group whose members exhibit problem behaviors?

12. Discuss the differences between reducing a person to a label (such as monopolist, help-rejecting complainer, the bore, and so on) and describing a specific behavior such as monopolizing. As a group leader, how can you encourage a member to recognize and deal with specific behaviors that are counterproductive to the progress of both the individual and the group?

13. Look over the list of "difficult group members" in the textbook. What kinds of problem behaviors or difficult members do you anticipate having the most difficulty with? Why? How might you typically respond?

14. There is a danger of pushing people too soon to give up a defense. Ask yourself if you are able to handle the reaction of a person who relinquishes a defense. For example, if you encourage a member to feel his anger instead of intellectualizing it, could you handle the possible explosive expression of his rage should he experience it fully? How can you determine whether or not you are competent to deal with what lies under a defense?

15. <u>Intellectualizing</u>. Assume that a person in the group you're leading talks about herself in a detached manner without emotion. How can you get her to express more affect? How could you help her to realize that she is intellectualizing?

16. <u>Questioning</u>. Monitor yourself as you lead a group. To what degree do you rely on questioning as a style in your group leading? Are you modeling a question/answer style for members?

    Consider telling people what you want from them instead of questioning them. What might happen if you <u>first</u> give your reasons for asking a question and <u>then</u> proceed to ask your question?

17. <u>Advise-giving</u>. Assume that a particular member continually gave advice every time a member talked about a struggle. How might you deal with such a member who typically tells others what they should do?

18. <u>Support versus Band-Aiding</u>.

    a. Imagine yourself explaining to a group the difference between genuine support and Band-Aiding. What would you tell them?

    b. Assume that a member gave support to everyone in the group, yet did not seem to be able to ask for support or handle it when it was directed toward her. What might be accomplished if you asked her to go around the room and complete any one of the following sentences? She would be asked to repeat the beginning of the same sentence and then complete it differently for each person in the group. Examples of these incomplete sentences are:

       You could support me by _____.

       If I couldn't support you, then _____.

       When I support you, I _____.

       If I give you support, _____.

    c. Now assume that you confront a person who interrupts and attempts to make others feel positive whenever they experience any discomfort or pain. The person snaps back with "I'm just trying to help. Why do you like to see people suffer?" How would you explain your rationale for implying that this person's support at that moment was not useful?

19. <u>Avoidance</u>. A member in a group you're leading not only avoids sharing himself in the group, but he is also successful in sidetracking what could be productive work of other members. How might you feel toward this kind of person? How would you deal with him?

20. <u>Dealing with silent members</u>.

    a. How can you determine the difference between silence that is productive and silence that is a defense?

b. Assume you have a silent member, one who rarely speaks even if she is encouraged to do so. What do you think would be the effects of the following strategies?

Call on her.

Ignore her.

Ask the group how they feel about her being silent.

Tell her that you are aware of her silence and that you are interested in what she has to say.

Pay close attention to her nonverbal messages.

Remind her of her contract to be a participant.

Ask her what stops her from speaking.

Ask her if her silence is satisfactory to her.

What other approaches would you consider?

c. How would you respond to a member who says "I learn a lot by listening. I'm the type who observes. I've never been much of a talker, but I do get something from listening to what others have to say."

21. <u>Monopolizing</u>. How would you respond to a person who dominated the group you were leading? What are some ways that you can think of to effectively work with a member who exhibits a great need for continual attention and whose attention-getting behavior disrupts the group?

22. <u>Storytelling</u>. Assume that you confront a person who is storytelling. He responds by saying "I'm hurt and confused. I felt I was risking a lot by telling you all about a private matter, and now you tell me that I'm storytelling. This makes me want to pull back and not say anything." What would you reply to him? What can you say about the difference between facilitative self-disclosure and pseudo-self-disclosure?

23. <u>Dependency</u>.

a. How would you respond to these forms of dependency?

The person who makes no move without consulting with you;

The person who seeks continual reassurance from everyone in the group;

The person who appears to listen and then proceeds to tell you why what you said won't work; and

The person who claims that he'd be utterly lost without this weekly group.

b. What might <u>you</u> as a group leader get from the dependency of clients on you? Which of your needs might foster their dependency?

24. <u>Hostile-aggressive behavior</u>. What would you do if you had an extremely hostile member (one who was indirect with his anger), whose effect on

the group was to close others up? What course of action would you take? Why?

25. In my experience in consulting and doing in-service workshops with people who lead groups, I've found that there is a tendency to focus on group members' behavior problems as a justification for the group's lack of success. What suggestions do you have that will enable you to focus on your own feelings and reactions? How can you avoid the pitfall of blaming "problem clients" for difficulties in a group, while leaving your own dynamics out of this process? How might you use members' problem behaviors to avoid your own responsibility? How might you creatively find avenues for expressing your own feelings and reactions toward problem behaviors you encounter in a group?

SELF-ASSESSMENT SCALE:
WHAT KIND OF GROUP MEMBER AM I?

I hope you have had some form of experience as a group member. If not, you can rate yourself on the following self-inventory in terms of your behavior in the class you're now in. These items refer to the role of group members, and they are geared to help you determine your strengths and weaknesses as a group member. I believe that one of the best ways of preparing for effective leadership is to first become an effective member.

After this inventory is completed, the class can break up into small groups; the groups can be composed of people who know each other best. Members of these groups should then assess one another's self-ratings. Discuss how you can become a better group member.

Rate yourself on a scale of from 1 to 5, with 1 being "almost never true of you" to 5 being "almost always true of you" as a group member.

___3___ 1. I am willing to raise personal concerns and explore them in the group.

___4___ 2. I am an active and contributing group member.

___4___ 3. I listen attentively to others, and I respond to them.

___2___ 4. I share my perceptions of others by giving them feedback of how I see them and how I am affected by them.

___2___ 5. I confront others with care, yet I do so directly.

___4___ 6. I'm willing to formulate specific goals and contracts when I am a member of a group.

___4___ 7. I'm willing to openly express my feelings about and reactions to what is occurring within the group.

___3___ 8. I serve as a positive model to others in the group.

___4___ 9. I am active in taking steps to create and maintain trust in the group.

17

__4__ 10. As a group participant, I give direct feedback to others, and I am open to considering feedback from them.

__3__ 11. I show that I am willing to put insights into action by practicing what I learn in the group in my life between sessions.

__2__ 12. I prepare myself for group by thinking about what I want from the sessions.

__4__ 13. I am willing to get involved in role-playing activities.

__3__ 14. I express persistent feelings I am having in group.

__4__ 15. I'm able to provide support to others in the group at appropriate times.

CHAPTER
4

Group Leadership

PROBLEMS AND ISSUES FACING
BEGINNING GROUP LEADERS

The corresponding chapter in the textbook deals with several common problems that group leaders (both those who are beginning and those who are experienced) typically face. Assume that you are now leading or coleading a
group (even though you may not have done so) and give your reactions to each
of the following situations. What do you imagine you'd think and feel in each
of these cases? Think about your possible courses of action, then discuss
these situations in your class/group and exchange ideas. There are plenty of
role-playing activities that can be generated from the material that follows.

1. Imagine yourself getting ready to colead your first group. What kind of
    anxiety would you experience? What would be your main concerns before
    you actually begin the first session? Assume you are meeting your co-
    leader an hour before the group meets. What things do you think you'd
    say to your coleader?

2. As a group leader there is a risk that you can disclose too little about
    yourself or that you can disclose too much. Let yourself imagine that
    you are not disclosing enough about yourself in a group. How do you see
    yourself? How are the members responding to you? How does your coleader
    react to you? What are you feeling now as you picture yourself as being
    an underdisclosing group leader? Now, imagine yourself to be an over-
    disclosing leader. In your mind see yourself talking too much about your-
    self, and in an inappropriate way. What are some things you might be
    saying in the group? How do you see yourself in this situation? How do
    the members react to you? How does your coleader react?

3. As a group leader, how do you decide when, what, and how to disclose in order to make self-disclosure facilitate, rather than interfere with, the group process? What are your guidelines for appropriate self-disclosure?

4. As you lead groups some members may develop transference toward you. This can consist of both positive and negative reactions to you, yet in many senses transference comprises feelings that members have or had toward significant people in their lives. Consider how you'd feel, what you'd think, how you'd respond, and what you might do as certain participants developed unrealistic views of you by casting you into each of the following fixed roles that met their needs:

    a. You are seen and treated as "the expert" and are constantly asked for advice.

    b. You are cast into the role of "authority figure." Certain members consistently feel either that you are judging them or that you are in some way exerting power over them.

    c. Some members see you as the "fully together person." They see you as being without any struggles.

    d. Certain members want you for a friend. They seek special attention from you and actively try to develop a friendship that extends beyond the group.

    e. You are seen as a potential lover, and you are the recipient of sexually seductive behaviors.

5. Your own objectivity can become distorted as a result of countertransference—feelings that are aroused in you toward certain clients and that tend to be based on unrecognized and unresolved personal issues. Put yourself into each of the following eight common countertransference situations. How would you fit into each of these situations? What are you aware of in yourself that might prevent you from focusing on the needs and best interests of group members?

    a. You have an inordinate need for reassurance and constant reinforcement; this includes the need to please all the members, to win their respect, to get them to approve of you, and to have them confirm you as a "superb leader."

    b. You see yourself in certain clients; you over-identify with some members to the extent that you take on their problems.

    c. You develop sexual and romantic feelings toward certain members; you engage in seductive behavior and allow your sexual attraction to become a central focus in the group.

    d. You give people advice in such a way that you tell others what to do based on your own needs and values.

e. You develop social relationships with some members outside of the group and find that you challenge them less during group sessions than other members.

f. You use power over members to prove your adequacy; you gain power through the use of certain highly directive techniques.

g. You attempt to persuade members to accept the values you hold; you are more interested in having members subscribe to your idea of the right way to live rather than letting members decide on their own values.

h. You see clearly the faults of members and use what they do or don't do to justify poor results in a group; at the same time you are blind to your own shortcomings or your part in the group process.

6. I believe that it is extremely important for group counselors to be aware of the personal traits and characteristics needed to become an effective leader. Select some of the following questions to discuss in your class or small group, and use them as a basis for self-reflection on effective leadership.

a. Why do you want to lead groups?

b. What do you have to offer as a group counselor?

c. What experiences have you had that you think will contribute to your success?

d. What shortcomings do you have that may limit your effectiveness as a leader?

e. Do you feel a sense of personal power in your own right, or do you depend on a role or position to give you power?

f. In what ways do you appreciate, value, respect, accept, and like yourself?

g. Do you see yourself as having courage? In what ways do you see courage as important for a group leader?

SKILLS IN OPENING AND CLOSING GROUP SESSIONS

I've observed that group leaders in training are frequently ineffective in opening and closing group meetings. For example, I've often seen leaders quickly focus on one group member at the beginning of a session, with no mention of the prior session. Members should at least be given a brief opportunity to share what they did in the way of practice outside of the group since the last session. Additionally, I find that it is useful to have each member briefly state what he or she wants from the upcoming session. Closing a group session should entail more than an abrupt announcement of the end of the meeting. It's more productive for the group leader to lead everyone in summarizing, integrating, and helping one another find ways of applying what they've learned in group to situations outside of group.

The following phrases, statements, and questions will give you some concrete tools that you can use to develop skills in opening and closing group sessions. Review this list frequently and experiment with parts of it at different times. Add your own opening and closing statements to help you get sessions moving well and end each of your meetings most effectively. I hope you will not employ these phrases mechanically; rather, you should find a way to introduce them in timely and appropriate ways. Eventually, some of these catalytic statements can become a natural part of your own leadership style.

Guidelines for Opening Group Sessions

• What do you want most from today's session?

• Last week we left off with _____.

• Did anyone have any afterthoughts about our last meeting?

• What did you do this week with what you learned in the last session?

• I'd like to go around the group and have each person complete the sentence: "Right now I am feeling _____."

• How would each of you like to be different today from how you were last session?

• Let's go around the group and have each person briefly say what his or her issues or agendas are for this particular session. What does each of you want from the group today?

• I'd like to share some of my thoughts regarding our last session.

• My expectations and hopes for this session are _____.

• If you did not participate in group today, how would that be for you?

• Let's all close our eyes. Realize that the next two hours are set aside for you. Ask yourself what you want and what you are willing to do in the group today to get it.

• How are each of you feeling about being here today?

• What are you willing to do to make this session productive?

• Could we have a report on how you are doing with your homework assignments?

• If you are here only because you are required to be, are you still willing to keep yourself open to getting something from the session?

• What would you have to lose if you participated?

• Before we begin I'd like each of you to sit quietly for a few minutes and do whatever is necessary to bring yourself into the room as fully as possible.

- Today marks the halfway point for our group. We have ten weeks remaining, and I'd like to discuss whether or not there is anything you'd like to change during the next ten weeks? How would each of you like to be different?

- Do any of you have any issues that you'd like to pursue?

- Is there any unfinished business from the last session that anyone wants to pursue?

- I'd like to go around the group and have each person finish the sentence: "Today I could be actively involved in group by _____."

What are some other phrases that you can add that you think are good leads for opening a particular group meeting?

_____

_____

_____

_____

_____

_____

Guidelines for Closing Group Sessions

- Before we end for today, is there anything anyone wants to say to anyone else in here?

- What, if anything, did you learn in today's session?

- What did you hear yourself or someone else say that seemed especially significant to you?

- If you were to summarize the key themes that were explored today, what would they be?

- What was it like for you to be here today?

- What would each of you like to do between now and the next session?

- Are there any issues anyone wants to work on at the next session?

- Could we quickly go around the group and have everyone say a few words about how this session was for him or her?

- I'd like to go around the group and have each of you complete the sentence: "One thing I need to practice outside of group is _____."

- Would each of you finish the sentence: "The thing I like best (or least) about this session was _____."?

- Let's spend the last ten minutes talking about your plans for the coming week. What is each of you willing to do outside of group?

- A homework assignment I'd like you to consider is _____.

- Does anyone want to give anyone else any feedback?

- Are there any changes you'd like to make in the group?

- What is each of you willing to say about each other's work?

- How is the group going for you so far?

- How are you for the group so far?

- We had quite an intense session today. I'm wondering if anyone feels "left hanging" and would like to say how he or she is feeling now.

- Several of you opened up some difficult problems. Although you don't have solutions to those problems, I hope you'll think about the feedback you received.

- Before we close, I'd like to share my own reactions concerning this session.

- I noticed that you were very quiet during the session. Are you willing to say how this meeting was for you?

- You opened up some pretty scarey feelings. You made important steps, and I'd like to go ahead in future sessions with what you are discovering.

- Many of you seemed rather lethargic today. I'd like to spend a few minutes before closing to talk about what this might mean.

List other phrases for closing a meeting.

_____

_____

_____

_____

_____

_____

EVALUATION AND CHECKLIST OF GROUP LEADER SKILLS

The textbook gives a brief but specific list of group-leader skills. The following form will help you review them and provide you with a self-evaluation rating scale. This can be considered a self-inventory that will give you, as a group leader, a set of criteria to assess many of your strengths and specific areas that need improvement. Read the brief description of each skill and then rate yourself on each one. Next, think about the questions listed under each skill; these will help you determine your level of skill development and examine your behavior as a leader. Ask yourself which skills you most need to develop or improve.

You can profit from this checklist/evaluation by reviewing it before and after group sessions. If you are working with a coleader, it could be very useful to have your coleader also rate you on each of these skills. These questions can also provide a systematic framework for exploring your level of skill development with fellow students and with your supervisor or instructor.

On these 21 skills, rate yourself on a five-point scale, using this code:

5 = This is done most of the time with a very high degree of competence.

4 = This is done much of the time with a high degree of competence.

3 = This is done sometimes with an adequate degree of competence.

2 = This is done occasionally with a relatively low level of competence.

1 = This is rarely demonstrated or done with an extremely low level of competence.

You are strongly encouraged to take this self-inventory at three points during the semester or quarter. The three blank spaces to the left of each number are for these three ratings. I recommend that you cover your previous ratings with a piece of paper so that you are not influenced by them. It would be ideal if you rate yourself (and have your coleader and supervisor rate you) about every five weeks. This will give you a regular pattern of your progress in developing group leadership skills. Above all, strive for the maximum degree of honesty with yourself as you complete this rating scale and as you reflect on the questions concerning each of these skills.

It is a good idea to circle the letter of the questions that are the most meaningful to you, as well as the questions that indicate the need for further skill development or special attention.

TO WHAT DEGREE DOES THE GROUP LEADER
DEMONSTRATE THE FOLLOWING:

_____ _____ _____ 1. Active listening: hearing, understanding, and communicating that one is doing this.
   a. How well do you listen to members?
   b. How attentive are you to nonverbal language?
   c. Are you able to detect incongruity between members' words and their nonverbal cues?
   d. Are you able to hear both direct and subtle messages?

25

      e. Do you teach members how to listen and to respond?

      f. Do you focus on <u>content</u> to the extent that you miss how a message is delivered?

_____ _____ _____ 2. <u>Restating</u>: capturing the essence of what is said in different words with the effect of adding meaning or clarifying meaning.

      a. Can you repeat the essence of what others say without becoming mechanical?

      b. Do your restatements add meaning to what was said by a member?

      c. Do your restatements eliminate ambiguity and give a sharper focus to what was said?

      d. Do you check with members to determine if they think your restatement is accurate?

_____ _____ _____ 3. <u>Clarifying</u>: focusing on underlying issues and assisting others to get a clearer picture of what they are thinking and/or feeling.

      a. Do your clarifying remarks assist members in sorting out conflicting feelings?

      b. Are you able to focus on underlying issues?

      c. Do members get a clearer focus on what they are thinking and feeling?

      d. Does your clarification lead to a deeper level of member self-exploration?

_____ _____ _____ 4. <u>Summarizing</u>: tying together loose ends, identifying common themes, and providing a picture of the directional trends of a group session.

      a. Do you use summarizing as a way to give more direction to a session?

      b. Do you tie together various themes in a group?

      c. Are you able to identify key elements of a session and present them as a summary of the proceedings at the end of a session?

_____ _____ _____ 5. <u>Questioning</u>: using questions to stimulate thought and action and to avoid a question/answer pattern of interaction between leader and member.

      a. Do you avoid overusing questioning as a leadership style?

      b. Do you use open-ended questions to encourage deeper exploration of issues?

      c. Do your questions lead clients in a definite direction? Do you have a hidden agenda? Do you have an expected answer?

      d. Do you model for members a low-level questioning style?

      e. Do you avoid bombarding members with questions that set up a question/answer format?

      f. Do you ask <u>what</u> and <u>how</u> questions, or <u>why</u> questions?

      g. Do you keep yourself hidden as a counselor through questioning instead of making statements?

_____ _____ _____ 6. Interpretation: explaining the meaning of behavior patterns within the framework of a theoretical system.
   a. Can you present your interpretations in a tentative way as a hunch or an hypothesis?
   b. Are your interpretations dogmatic and authoritarian? Do you have a need to convince members of what you see as "truth?"
   c. Do you have a tendency to rescue members from difficult feelings too quickly through the use of interpretations?
   d. Are you conscious of appropriateness and timing in making interpretations?
   e. Do you encourage members to provide their own meaning of their behavior?
   f. Do you invite other members to make interpretations?

_____ _____ _____ 7. Confrontation: challenging members in a direct way on discrepancies and in such a manner that they will tend to react nondefensively to the confrontation.
   a. How do you confront members? What are the effects of your confrontations, generally?
   b. What kind of model do you provide for confronting others with care and respect?
   c. As a result of your confrontations, are members encouraged to look at discrepancies in a nondefensive manner?
   d. Do you confront people about their unused strengths?
   e. Are you sensitive to the timing and appropriateness of your confrontations?
   f. Are your confrontations related to specific behavior, rather than being judgmental?

_____ _____ _____ 8. Reflecting feelings: mirroring what others appear to be feeling without being mechanical.
   a. Do you reflect feelings accurately?
   b. Do your reflections foster increased contact and involvement?
   c. Do your reflections help members clarify what they are feeling?

_____ _____ _____ 9. Support: offering some form of positive reinforcement at appropriate times in such a way that it has a facilitating effect.
   a. Do you recognize the progress that members make?
   b. Do you build on the strengths and gains made by members?
   c. Do you make use of positive reinforcement and encouragement?
   d. Does your support allow and encourage members to both express and explore their feelings? Or does your support tend to bolster up members and aid them in avoiding intense feelings?

_____ _____ _____ 10. <u>Empathy</u>: intuitively sensing the subjective world of others in a group, being able to adopt the frame of reference of others, and communicating this understanding to clients so that they feel understood.
  a. Are your life experiences diverse enough to provide a basis for understanding the subjective world of a range of clients?
  b. Are you able to demonstrate the ability to adopt the internal frame of reference of the client and communicate to that person that you do deeply understand?
  c. Are you able to maintain your separate identity at the same time as you empathize with others?

_____ _____ _____ 11. <u>Facilitating</u>: helping members to clarify their own goals and take the steps to reach them.
  a. How much do you encourage member interaction?
  b. Do you foster autonomy among the members by assisting them to accept an increasing degree of responsibility for directing their group?
  c. Are you successful in teaching members how to focus on themselves?
  d. Do you foster the spirit in members to identify and express whatever they are feeling as it relates to the here-and-now process of group interaction?

_____ _____ _____ 12. <u>Initiating</u>: demonstrating an active stance in intervening in a group at appropriate times.
  a. Do you have the skills to get group sessions started in an effective manner?
  b. Are you able to initiate new work with others once a given member's work is concluded?
  c. Do you take active steps to prevent the group from floundering in unproductive ways?
  d. Are you able to get interaction going among members or between leader and members?
  e. Do you avoid initiating to the degree that members assume a passive stance?

_____ _____ _____ 13. <u>Goal setting</u>: being able to cooperatively work with members so that there is an alignment between member goals and leader goals, and being able to assist members in establishing concrete goals.
  a. Do you help members to establish clear and specific goals?
  b. Are you able to help members clarify their own goals?
  c. Do you encourage members to develop contracts and homework assignments as ways of obtaining their goals?
  d. Do you impose your goals on the members without making them partners in the goal selection process?

28

_____ _____ _____ 14. Feedback: giving information to members in such a way that they can use it to make constructive behavior changes.
   a. Do you continually give concrete and useful feedback to members, and do you encourage members to do this for one another?
   b. Is your feedback both honest and personal?
   c. Do you teach members to sift through feedback and ultimately decide what they will do with this information?
   d. Do you offer feedback that relates to both the strengths and weaknesses of members?
   e. How do members typically react when you give them feedback?

_____ _____ _____ 15. Suggestion: offering information or possibilities for action that can be used by members in making independent decisions.
   a. Can you differentiate between suggesting and prescribing?
   b. Do you give too many suggestions, and are they just ways of providing quick solutions for every problem a member presents?
   c. Do you rush in too quickly to give advice or information, or do you encourage group members to provide themselves with possible courses of action?
   d. Do you invite others in the group to offer suggestions for members to consider?
   e. Do your directions and suggestions actually restrict members to becoming autonomous?

_____ _____ _____ 16. Protecting: actively intervening to insure that members will be safeguarded from unnecessary psychological risks.
   a. Do you take measures to safeguard members from unnecessary risks?
   b. Do you show good judgment in risky situations?
   c. Do you intervene when members are being treated unfairly or are being pressured by others?
   d. Do you talk with members about the possible psychological risks that are involved in group participation?

_____ _____ _____ 17. Self-disclosure: willingly sharing with members any persistent personal reactions that relate to the here-and-now occurrences in the group.
   a. What is your style of self-disclosure? Are you aloof? Do you remain hidden behind a role? Do you model appropriate self-disclosure?
   b. What impact do your self-disclosures tend to have on the group?
   c. Are you willing to reveal your present feelings and thoughts to members when it is appropriate?

_____ _____ _____ 18. Modeling: demonstrating to members desired behaviors that can be practiced both during and between group sessions.
  a. What kind of model are you for your clients?
  b. What specific behaviors and attitudes do you model?
  c. Are you doing in your own life what you ask the members in your group to do?
  d. What might the members of your group know about you by observing your actions in the group?

_____ _____ _____ 19. Use of silence: dealing effectively with silence and the meaning underlying it.
  a. Are you intimidated by silence in the group?
  b. Can you differentiate between useful silences and silences that are a form of resistance?
  c. What do you do with silence? Ignore it? Encourage members to look for its meaning? Use a technique to get action in the group? Ask questions?
  d. Do you tend to intervene quickly to break silences because you are uncomfortable?

_____ _____ _____ 20. Blocking: being able to intervene effectively, without attacking anyone, when members engage in counterproductive behaviors in group.
  a. Do you take active steps to intervene when there are counterproductive forces within a group?
  b. Do you generally block the following behaviors when you are aware of them in a group: Scapegoating? Group pressure? Questioning? Storytelling? Gossiping?
  c. Do you block counterproductive behavior in a firm yet sensitive manner?

_____ _____ _____ 21. Terminating: creating a climate that encourages members to continue working after sessions.
  a. Do you attempt to get members to translate what they are learning in group to their everyday lives?
  b. Do you assist members in reviewing and integrating their experiences?
  c. Do you create a climate wherein members are encouraged to continue to think and act after sessions?

SUGGESTIONS FOR USING THE GROUP-LEADER
EVALUATION FORM

Obviously, all of the preceding 21 items are not merely skills to learn. Many of them represent attitudes related to your leadership effectiveness; some represent personal characteristics that many writers think are ideal qualities of group leaders. Again, you are encouraged to complete this self-evaluation inventory three times during the course and to use it when you actually lead groups.

Finally, I recommend that you look over the preceding list of group-leader skills and circle the numbers of those items that are most important to you. Then use the following guide to summarize your major strengths, the areas you most need to improve, and the areas that you would like to explore more fully in class. Also, it could be valuable to make comparisons of these ratings; for example, how does your self-rating compare with ratings by your supervisor, your coleader, and the members of your group?

1. Some areas where I feel particularly strong are: _____

_____

_____

_____

_____

_____

2. Areas that need improvement most are: _____

_____

_____

_____

_____

_____

3. Some specific steps I can begin to take now to work toward improving these skills, attitudes, behaviors, and personal characteristics are:

_____

_____

_____

_____

_____

_____

4. In comparing my self-evaluation with others' evaluations of me, I

found: _____

_____

_____

_____

_____

_____

5. One way that I can continue to honestly engage in ongoing self-

appraisal is by: _____

_____

_____

_____

_____

_____

PART
II

Theoretical Approaches
to Group Counseling

CHAPTER

5

The Psychoanalytic Approach

PRECHAPTER PRIMERS AND SELF-INVENTORIES

General Directions

The purpose of the primers and self-inventories is to identify and clarify your attitudes and beliefs about the different theoretical approaches to group therapy. Each of the statements on these inventories is <u>true</u> from the perspective of the particular theory in question. You decide the degree to which you agree/disagree with these statements. Complete each self-inventory <u>before</u> you read the corresponding textbook chapter. Respond to each statement, giving the intial response that most clearly identifies how you think or feel. Then, after reading the chapter, look over your responses to see if you want to modify them in any way. These self-inventories will help you express your views and will prepare you to actively read and think about the ideas you'll encounter in each of the chapters on theory.

I suggest that you go over your completed inventories and mark those items you would like to discuss; then bring your inventories to class and compare your positions with the views of others. Such comparisons can stimulate debate and help get the class involved in the topics to be discussed.

Using the following code, write the number of the response that most closely reflects your viewpoint on the line to the left of each statement:

5 = I <u>strongly agree</u> with this statement.

4 = I <u>agree</u>, in most respects, with this statement.

3 = I am <u>undecided</u> in my opinion about this statement.

2 = I <u>disagree</u>, in most respects, with this statement.

1 = I <u>strongly disagree</u> with this statement.

34

PRECHAPTER PRIMER AND SELF-INVENTORY FOR THE
PSYCHOANALYTIC APPROACH TO GROUPS

_____ 1. The key to understanding human behavior is understanding the unconscious.

_____ 2. In group work, it is particularly important to focus on experiences from the first five years of life, because the roots of present conflicts usually lie there.

_____ 3. Group work should encourage participants to relive significant relationships, and the group should become a symbolic family so that members can work through these early relationships.

_____ 4. Insight, understanding, and working through repressed material should be given primary focus in group therapy.

_____ 5. Free association, dream work, analysis, and interpretation are essential components of effective group work.

_____ 6. Transference should be encouraged in a group, because it is through this process that members come to an understanding of unresolved conflicts in certain relationships.

_____ 7. Because of the reconstructive element of analytic group work, the process should be a long-term one.

_____ 8. An understanding of the forms resistance takes is essential for the group leader.

_____ 9. Group leaders must be continually aware of ways that their feelings (countertransference) can affect the group.

_____ 10. Effective therapy cannot occur unless the causes of a client's problems are identified.

SUMMARY OF THE BASIC ASSUMPTIONS AND KEY CONCEPTS
OF THE PSYCHOANALYTIC APPROACH TO GROUP WORK

1. The human personality is basically determined by unconscious motivations, irrational forces, sexual and aggressive impulses, and early childhood experiences. Understanding the unconscious is the key to understanding human behavior.

2. Normal personality development is based on a successful resolution of conflicts at various stages of psychosexual development.

3. Psychoanalytic therapists pay particular attention to the unconscious and the early developmental years as crucial determinants of personality and behavior.

4. Because it is necessary for clients to relive and reconstruct their past and work through repressed conflicts in order to understand how the un-

STAGES OF DEVELOPMENT OF THE PSYCHOANALYTIC GROUP

Dimension	Initial Stage	Working Stage	Final Stage
Key developmental tasks and goals	Key task is uncovering and exploring unconscious material. Focus is on historical causes of present behavior. Unconscious processes are made conscious by promoting freedom to express any thought, fantasy, and feeling.	The group resembles the original family, allowing members to relive their childhoods and to get to the roots of their conflicts. Key tasks include: recalling of early childhood experiences and reworking of past traumas. The basic work entails recognizing and working through resistances and transferences. Multiple transferences occur in the group; members become aware of past relationships that are brought into the present situation in the group.	Key task is the development of insight into causes of problems. Analysis and interpretation of transference continues. Focus is on the conscious personal action that members can take and on social integration. Main goals are for members to analyze and resolve their own transferences and avoid countertransferences toward other members, and to work through the repetition of behavior from early years.
Role of group leader and tasks	Leader offers support and creates a permissive and nonstructured climate. Leader's tasks include: setting limits, interpreting, and getting a sense of the members' character structures and patterns of defense.	Leader makes timely interpretations that lead to insight; helps members deal with anxiety constructively; is aware of countertransference; and helps members deal effectively with resistances and transferences in the group.	Leader relinquishes much of the leadership functions to allow the members a greater degree of independence; guides the members to fuller awareness and social integration.
Role of group members	Members build rapport by reporting dreams and fantasies. They are expected to free associate with one another's dreams. They are expected to work through resistances that prevent unconscious material from becoming conscious.	Members produce material in a free-floating manner; they ventilate and express feelings over past traumas. Emphasis is on working through transferences with leader and members. Members function as adjunct therapists by saying whatever comes to their minds uncensored about others; they also make interpretations for others.	Resistances and transferences are worked through, and focus is on self-interpretation and on reality testing. Members become able to spot their own transference figures and relationships; they also contribute to the interpretation of the transferences of others.

36

Techniques	Individual sessions are used to create readiness for a group. "Go-around" technique is used as a free-association device, where members respond spontaneously to each other. Initial resistances are dealt with.	Main techniques that are used include: free association, interpretation, analysis of resistance and transference, interpretation and analysis of dreams, use of alternate sessions and use of pregroup and postgroup sessions.	Alternate sessions and the pregroup meeting or postgroup meeting may continue.

Reactions: Summarize your reactions to the psychoanalytic perspective of group developmental stages. What do you like most? Least? What aspects of this approach would you incorporate into your style of leadership?

Questions: What questions about psychoanalytic group therapy would you most like to raise and explore?

conscious affects one now, psychoanalytic group therapy is intensive and generally involves a long-term commitment.

5. A major portion of group work consists of dealing with resistance, work-ing through transference, experiencing catharsis, developing insight and self-understanding, and learning the relationship between past experi-ences and their effect on current development.

6. Analytically oriented group practitioners tend to remain relatively anonymous and encourage group members to project onto them the feelings that they have had toward the significant people in their lives. The analysis and interpretation of transference leads to insight and person-ality change. (Some analytically oriented therapists do not always remain anonymous, however; they may respond to members in personal ways.)

7. Some of the unique advantages of the analytic group-therapy approach are: members are able to experience relationships that are similar to their own family relationships and thus reexperience some of those early rela-tionships; there are opportunities for multiple transferences; members can gain insight into their defenses and resistances more dramatically than they can in individual therapy; and dependency on the authority of the therapist is lessened, for members get feedback from other members.

EXERCISES AND ACTIVITIES FOR THE
PSYCHOANALYTIC APPROACH TO GROUPS

Rationale

In this workbook I present a wide range of exercises that are based on particular therapeutic models. Let me emphasize that strict practitioners of each approach may disagree that these exercises present commonly used tech-niques. My aim is to use the concepts of each therapeutic model to build exercises that you can practice, modify, and adapt to fit your needs. I hope you will develop your own techniques for use in your own group work.

For the exercises in this section, I've selected several group techniques that are based on conventional psychoanalytic concepts and procedures and modified them considerably in the hope that you will be able to apply some of them in your group work. The following exercises are geared to stimulate your thinking on issues such as the value of working with the past, being open to what you can learn from the unconscious, experimenting with tech-niques like free association and dream work, and increasing your appreciation of the importance of central concepts such as resistance, transference, and countertransference. In my opinion, regardless of their theoretical orienta-tion, group practitioners must understand these concepts. As you work through these exercises in your class/group, remain open to ways you can incorporate some of them into your style of leading groups.

Exercises

1. The alternate session. It is a common practice for psychoanalytic groups that meet on a weekly basis with a leader to supplement their sessions with meetings without a formal leader. (Refer to the textbook for a dis-cussion of the rationale of leaderless meetings on a regular basis.) If

38

you are in a group (as a part of the experience for this course) that meets with a leader, consider having some meetings where the leadership could be shifted among the members. For example, two of you could colead the group using the therapeutic model that you are studying that week. Discuss the values and the problems of self-directed or leaderless groups.

2. Working with your past. The analytic approach is based on the assumption that past experiences play a vital role in shaping one's current personality. The following short exercises/questions are designed to assist you in remembering and exploring in your group selected dimensions of your past.

   a. Recall and reconstruct some childhood experiences. Examining pictures of yourself as a child, interviewing people who knew you well, looking over diaries, and so on can be useful means of stimulating recall. Share in your group some of what you consider to be the most significant influences from your past. How have these factors contributed to the person you are now?

   b. Assign roles to various members of your group and have them be your family. Re-create a typical family situation by coaching them. What impact has this situation had on you?

   c. Write an outline (such as you might find in the table of contents) of a book that you could write about your life. Pay attention mainly to chapter headings. Examples might include: "The child who was never allowed to be a child"; "A time of abandonment"; "My most joyous memories"; "Dreams I had as a child"; "The things I wanted to be as a child." You could also write the Preface to this book about your life and include an acknowledgment section. Who are the people you'd most want to acknowledge as having a significant impact on your life? In what ways have they made a difference?

   d. In the outline for the book on your life, include a chapter where you rewrite your past the way you would have wanted it to be. Share your ideas for this chapter with your group.

   e. Make a list of your current struggles and see if you can trace the origins of these conflicts to childhood events.

   f. Freud believed that the events of the first five years of life are crucial determinants of our personalities. What can you find out about this time in your life? What hunches do you have about the effect of your early years on the person you now are?

3. Free association. A key method of unlocking the unconscious is free association; the therapist asks clients to clear their minds of day-to-day thoughts and simply report in a spontaneous way whatever comes to mind. This "flowing" with feelings and associations can tap underlying unconscious material. When clients block and censor what they are saying, this is seen as resistance to getting into contact with the unconscious.
   There are several ways to use free association in a group. For example, members can be encouraged to say whatever comes to them, regardless of how appropriate or meaningful it may seem. Often participants censor their contributions; they rehearse what they will say for fear that "it

won't come out right." Some members agonize over what to bring up in a group and exactly how to present a personal issue.

Participants can also be asked to go around to the other group members and say the first thing that they think as they face each person. A variation of this is going around to each person and quickly completing sentences. For example, if a woman discloses in group that she finds it difficult to share personal matters because she doesn't trust the men in the group, it can be suggested that she go before each man and complete a sentence such as: "One thing I least trust about you is ____"; or "If I open myself up in here then you ____"; or "When I think of trusting you ____." She can continue to make associations with whatever develops from completing each sentence. By doing this she increases her chances of overcoming blocks and thus makes contact with significant unconscious material.

During a free-association process, group leaders might identify repressed and blocked material. The sequence of associations gives leaders cues to anxiety-arousing material, and they can begin making connections and then interpreting the meaning of these associations to the client. For example, in the woman's case above, the leader may see some connections between her present distrust of men with a series of instances where her father violated her trust. She may have come to the conclusion, "If you can't trust your own father, then what man can you trust?"

It might also be a productive exercise in your group to make up your own incomplete sentences, finish them, and then find ways to free associate with what seems to be significant material. For example, you might work with sentences such as:

• When I'm in this group I feel _____.

• One way I attempt to avoid things in this group is by _____.

• One fear I have is _____.

• One way I isolate myself at times is by _____.

One more variation of a free-association exercise is to select an object in the room you are in and "become this object." Each person takes an inanimate object and gives that object voice, character, and life. As you become this object, interact with other members in the group as others are portraying their objects. After you've done this for a time, discuss what this process was like. What significance is there in the kind of objects people selected?

4. Dream work. Report the key elements of one of your dreams to your group. You might try the following suggestions as a way of learning something about yourself through your dreams.

    a. Select any part of your dream and free associate with that part. Say as many words as fast as you can without censoring them. After you've done this, see what your free-association work tells you.

    b. Give an initial interpretation of your dream. What themes or patterns do you see?

40

c. Next, ask group members to give their interpretations of your dream. What do they think your dream means?

d. If they want to, other group members can free associate with any parts of your dream.

You might want to begin keeping a dream journal. Write down your dreams. Record what you remember. Then look at the patterns of your dreams and interpret their meaning.

5. Resistance. Brainstorm all the possible ways you might resist in a group. What resistances have you experienced to simply getting into a group? List some avoidance patterns that you have seen in yourself in group.
    Next, discuss some possible causes of resistance in group members. What might they be defending themselves against? What are some ways that you can think of to help group members recognize and work through resistances that could prevent them from effectively working in a group?

6. Transference. A central concept in analytic group therapy is the identification and working through of transference. To get some idea of this process, try some of these exercises in your group.

    a. Go around to each person in the group. Does anyone remind you of a significant person in your life? Discuss the similarities. (Select people who caused especially strong reactions in you.)

    b. You can also explore possible transferences that occur outside of the group. Have you ever experienced strong, immediate, and even irrational reactions to a person you hardly knew? Discuss what you can learn about unfinished business from your past by focusing on such occurrences.

7. Countertransference.

    a. What kind of clients do you think you'd have the most difficulty working with in a group? Why? How do you imagine that you'd handle a client who had very strong negative feeling toward you, especially if you felt that these feelings were inappropriate and a function of transference? How might you handle a group member with the same degree of intense feelings (also transference) if they were positive ones? What personal needs or unresolved conflicts within you could make it difficult for you to work with members with either positive or negative transference?

    b. Select a client who you think is a difficult group member and who you anticipate will cause you problems. Become this client. Take on this person's characteristics as fully as you can. Others in the group can function as members and one person can be the group leader and attempt to work with you. (Several members might want to get some experience being the leader and working with you, each using a different approach.) After you've had a chance to take on the role of this "problem member" for awhile, explore what this experience was like for you. How did the other members respond to you? How did the group leader respond to you?

c. Make up a list of specific problems that you might have that could interfere with your effectiveness in leading groups. For example, you may have an extreme need to be appreciated, which could determine your leadership style. You may have unresolved sexual conflicts, dependency needs, or exaggerated needs for power. Identify one area that you think you most need to explore as a potential barrier to effective leadership. Discuss this problem with your group. Although it may be unrealistic to expect a solution, you can talk about steps you could take to work on this problem.

8. <u>Being a group member</u>. What do you imagine that it would be like for you to be a member of an ongoing analytic group? What issues do you think you'd want to pursue in such a group? What kind of member do you think you'd be?

9. <u>Role of group leader</u>. Review the section in the textbook on the role of the analytic group leader. If you were to work within the framework of this model, what would this be like for you? Could you function within this model if it were your primary orientation? Why or why not?

10. <u>Personal critique</u>. Devote some time to a personal evaluation of the strengths and weaknesses of the analytic approach to group therapy. What specific techniques do you think are valuable? Why? What concepts could you draw on from this model in your work with groups, regardless of your orientation? What are the major contributions of the analytic model? What are the major limitations? With what kind of population do you think this model would be most appropriate? Least appropriate? Discuss how the psychoanalytic theory forms the basis on which most of the other theories have developed—either as extensions of the model or as reactions against it.

6

Psychoanalytic Adaptations: The Developmental Model and the Adlerian Approach

PRECHAPTER PRIMER AND SELF-INVENTORY FOR
PSYCHOANALYTIC ADAPTATIONS

Directions: Refer to page 34 for general directions. Indicate your position on each statement, using the following code:

5 = I strongly agree with this statement.

4 = I agree, in most respects, with this statement.

3 = I am undecided in my opinion about this statement.

2 = I disagree, in most respects, with this statement.

1 = I strongly disagree with this statement.

The first five items on this inventory are drawn from Erikson's stages of human development.

_____ 1. Unresolved conflicts in an earlier developmental stage have an influence on later stages.

_____ 2. Developmental crises occur in each period of life.

_____ 3. Group leaders must have an understanding of what tasks are important at various stages of group development to function effectively.

_____ 4. Group counseling is a useful approach in helping members learn about the universality of their conflicts.

STAGES OF DEVELOPMENT OF THE ADLERIAN GROUP

Dimension	Initial Stage	Working Stage	Final Stage
Key developmental tasks and goals	Central developmental tasks are: establishing empathy and creating acceptance; setting goals and making commitments; understanding one's current life-style and exploring one's premises and assumptions.	Members are helped to understand their beliefs, feelings, motives, and goals; they develop insight into their mistaken goals and self-defeating behaviors; they work through interpersonal conflicts, and they explore the beliefs behind their feelings. A goal is to create meaning and significance in life. Through group interaction, one's basic values and life-style become evident.	This is a time when members explore multiple alternatives to problems and make a commitment to change; members translate insights into action and make new decisions. A goal is to facilitate members' awareness of their mistaken notions through observation of fellow group members and reality testing.
Role of group leader and tasks	Main goal of the group leader is to establish a collaborative relationship and to decide with clients on the goals of the group. Leader's tasks include: providing encouragement, offering support and tentative hypotheses of behavior, helping members to assess and clarify their problems. Role of leader is to observe social context of behavior in group; to model attentive listening, caring, sincerity, and confrontation. Leader helps members to recognize and utilize their strengths.	Functions of leader at the working stage include: interpreting early recollections and family patterns; helping members identify basic mistakes; helping members become aware of their own unique life-styles; challenging members to deal with life tasks; helping members summarize and integrate what they've learned so that they can make new plans.	At the final stage the focus is on reeducation. Leader helps members challenge attitudes and encourages members to take risks and experiment with new behavior by translating their new ideas into actual behavior outside of the group.
Role of group members	Members state their goals and establish contracts. They are expected to be active in the group and begin to assume responsibility for the ways they want to change. Members begin to work on trust issues, which are important in the encouragement process and in developing good morale within the group.	Members become increasingly aware of their life-styles. They analyze the impact of family constellation; they also begin to recognize that they are responsible for their own behavior. Members provide support and challenge others so that they can explore their basic inferiority feelings. Participants learn to believe in themselves.	Members are expected to establish realistic goals. They see new options and more functional alternatives. They learn problem-solving and decision-making skills. This is a time of reorientation. Members encourage one another to redirect their goals along realistic lines.

Techniques	Basic listening skills are crucial at this time. Analysis and assessment of one's life-style and how it affects current functioning are conducted. Other techniques include questioning, reflection, and clarification.	Some of the techniques used at this stage are: confrontation; interpretation; modeling; paraphrasing; encouragement; "catching oneself" in old patterns; acting "as if"; and teaching.	Basic procedures at the final stage consist of encouraging members to act and to change. Contracts are reestablished, and role-playing techniques are used to help members reorient their goals. There is a continuation of the encouragement process.

Reactions: Summarize your reactions to the Adlerian perspective on group developmental stages. What do you like most? Least? What aspects of this approach would you incorporate into your style of group leadership?

Questions: What questions about Adlerian group therapy would you most like to raise and explore?

_____ 5. The quality of love we receive as children influences our later outlook on life.

The next five items on this inventory are drawn from the Adlerian approach to group work.

_____ 6. Recalling one's earliest memories is an extremely important group-work technique.

_____ 7. People have a basic need to be superior—that is, to overcome feelings of inferiority.

_____ 8. Each person develops a unique life style, which should be examined in group sessions.

_____ 9. The group counselor's and the group member's goals must concur.

_____ 10. An analysis of each member's family constellation is essential to successful group work.

SUMMARY OF BASIC ASSUMPTIONS AND KEY CONCEPTS
OF THE ADLERIAN APPROACH TO GROUPS

1. The underlying assumptions of the Adlerian approach are: Humans are primarily social beings, motivated by social forces; they are shaped largely by social interactions; Conscious, not unconscious, processes determine personality and behavior; People are creative, active, and autonomous beings, not the victims of fate.

2. All people have basic feelings of inferiority that motivate them to strive for superiority, mastery, power, and perfection.

3. People seek to overcome helplessness through compensation. People's lifestyles comprise unique behaviors and habits they develop in striving for power, meaning, and personal goals; their life-styles, which are formed early in life as compensations for specific feelings of inferiority, also shape their views of the world and of themselves.

4. Therapists should encourage group members to become actively involved with other people and develop new life-styles through relationships.

5. Therapists should challenge clients to have faith and hope and develop the courage to face life actively and choose the kind of life they want. This is done largely by living as if we were the way we want to be.

EXERCISES AND ACTIVITIES FOR THE
ALDERIAN APPROACH TO GROUPS

1. Adlerians use a technique known as "the question." This consists of asking a client "How would you be different if _____?" The end of the sentence refers to being free of a problem or a symptom. For example, if you were troubled with migraine headaches, you would be asked how you'd

be different if you no longer had these headaches. Apply this question to a specific problem you have. Explore how your life might be different without this problem. How do you think your problem may be useful to you? Are you "rewarded" for some of your symptoms?

2. What are some of your earliest memories? Describe them in your group. Are they mainly joyful or painful memories? What value do you see in the Adlerian technique of having clients recall their earliest memories? Can you think of ways to use this technique in groups you may lead?

3. Adlerians place emphasis on birth order and family constellation. Share with your group members what it was like to be the first-born child, or the last-born, or the middle child, or the only child. What does your group think are the advantages and disadvantages of each of these positions? Discussing these topics can help group members get acquainted with each other, as well as stir up old memories.

4. According to Adler, we all strive for superiority to compensate for inferiority. How does this apply to you? In what ways do you feel inferior? Do you see yourself as having developed certain strengths that characterize the way you present yourself to others? In describing your lifestyle consider such questions as: What makes you unique? How do you strive for power? When do you feel the most powerful? What are the goals that you most strive for? What do you most often tell others about yourself on a first meeting? How do you typically present yourself?

5. Adlerian therapists often ask group members to live "_as if_" they were the person they wanted to be. For example, you may want to be far more creative than you are now. Assume that you were more creative, and then describe yourself to your group. What are some ways that you can think of to use this "as if" technique in a group? What value do you see in it?

6. Adlerians center on "basic mistakes," or faulty assumptions that people make about themselves. These mistaken ideas lead to self-defeating behavior. For example, you may believe that to feel successful you must be perfect. Since you'll never feel like you're perfect, you will constantly put yourself under needless stress and experience little joy over any accomplishments. Select what you consider to be one faulty assumption that you have made about yourself or the world. Discuss in your group how this affects you. If you were to change this assumption, how might your life be different?

7. What is your personal evaluation of the Adlerian approach to group therapy? What do you see as the major strengths and limitations of the model? What concepts do you like most? Like least? Which Adlerian group-therapy methods would you use?

CHAPTER
7

Psychodrama

PRECHAPTER PRIMER AND SELF-INVENTORY
FOR PSYCHODRAMA

<u>Directions</u>: Refer to page 34 for general directions. Indicate your position on each statement, using the following code:

5 = I <u>strongly agree</u> with this statement.

4 = I <u>agree</u>, in most respects, with this statement.

3 = I am <u>undecided</u> in my opinion about this statement.

2 = I <u>disagree</u>, in most respects, with this statement.

1 = I <u>strongly disagree</u> with this statement.

_____ 1. There is therapeutic value in releasing pent-up feelings, even if this process does not lead to changing external situations.

_____ 2. Much can be learned from acting out one's conflicts, rather than merely talking about them.

_____ 3. The use of fantasy techniques in a group can increase members' awareness of themselves.

_____ 4. Group members can learn a great deal about themselves by observing and experiencing the psychodramas of other members.

_____ 5. It is important to "warm up" a group before moving into action.

_____ 6. Role playing one's own role <u>and</u> the role of a significant other person can increase one's awareness of oneself.

_____ 7. After intensive group work, members should share their feelings and discuss how they perceive the work.

_____ 8. A group leader should both encourage catharsis and help members understand emotional experiences.

_____ 9. Group members (protagonists) should always have the right to choose what conflict they will portray, and they should have the right to say that they do not want to move in a given direction.

_____ 10. Unless a group is cohesive, it is unlikely that members will risk role playing important problems.

SUMMARY OF THE BASIC ASSUMPTIONS AND
KEY CONCEPTS OF PSYCHODRAMA

1. Psychodrama frees people from old feelings so that they are able to develop new ways of responding to problems. Spontaneity, creativity, fantasy, and role playing are essential elements of psychodrama.

2. Psychodrama emphasizes enacting or reenacting events (anticipated or past) as though they were occurring now.

3. Feelings are released; participants gain insight and are provided with the opportunity to test reality. Group members suggest alternatives for action.

4. The psychodrama leader's tasks include being a producer, catalyst/facilitator, and observer/analyzer.

5. A basic assumption underlying psychodrama is that members of the group can benefit therapeutically in vicarious ways by identifying with a protagonist in a psychodrama.

6. Psychodrama has three phases: the warm-up process, the action phase, and the discussion phase.

STAGES OF DEVELOPMENT OF THE PSYCHODRAMA GROUP

Dimension	Initial Stage	Working Stage	Final Stage
Key developmental tasks and goals	The key task of the initial stage is the warm-up, which fosters spontaneity. This warm-up period develops a readiness to participate in the experience. Emphasis is on forming common bonds by identifying common experiences.	A major task of psychodrama is to facilitate expression of feelings in a spontaneous and dramatic way through role playing. Full expression of conflicts leads to new awareness of problems. During this phase a corrective emotional experience occurs through enactment and catharsis that tends to lead to insight. Reality testing can follow, using a variety of techniques.	Major tasks of this phase are: working through conflict situations by behavioral practice and by getting feedback; developing a sense of mastery over certain problems; receiving support from group, and integrating what is learned into life outside the group.
Role of director and tasks	The director introduces the nature and purpose of psychodrama and warms up the audience (group) using techniques. Members are briefly interviewed and asked what kind of situation they would be willing to work on. A protagonist is selected. Director's main task is to create a climate of support and prepare the group drama. Director may select a theme (such as loneliness, dealing with intimacy, and so on) that the group can focus on.	During this phase the director's task is to encourage members to enact scenes involving conflicts. The emphasis is on action, keeping the members focused on the present, and helping them to fully express feelings. The director facilitates and interprets the action and encourages spontaneity and expression. The director brings other members forward to take the parts of other significant figures in the protagonist's drama. The director helps these auxiliary egos learn their roles.	After the main action, the director helps the protagonist integrate what has occurred. Director asks for feedback and support from other members; in this way, all the members of the group get involved in the psychodrama. Care is taken so that those who participated in the psychodrama are not left hanging. Director may summarize the session and help everyone to integrate the psychodramatic occurrences.
Role of group members	The members discuss goals, get acquainted with one another, and participate in exercises to get them focused. Members may decide on a theme of common interest, which in turn leads to the selection of a protagonist. Members decide what personal issues they will explore.	Members define in concrete terms a situation to be enacted; they reconstruct an event from past or anticipated in the future that causes anxiety. The members fantasize and express themselves as fully as possible, both verbally and nonverbally. Members serve as auxiliary egos for the protagonist.	Members share with the protagonist feelings they had as the enactment took place. The sharing is done in a personal way, not an analytical way. Members give feedback to the protagonist, and they offer support. Members share the personal experiences that the psychodrama reminded them of.

50

| Techniques | The warm-up period may be directed or undirected. Warm-up techniques include the use of guided fantasy, dance, and music, the use of artistic materials, the sharing of drawings, and brief interviews of each member. | A wide range of action-oriented techniques are used to enhance psychodrama. These techniques include self-presentation, presentation of the other, role reversal, soliloquy, doubling, the mirror technique, dream work, and future projection. | After the action phase of a psychodrama, certain closure techniques may be used such as sharing techniques, the magic shop, feedback, repeating the drama with new approaches, and discussing alternative behaviors and possible solutions to problems. |

Reactions: Summarize your reactions to the psychodramatic perspective on group developmental stages. What do you like most? Least? What aspects of this approach would you incorporate into your style of leadership?

Questions: What questions about psychodrama would you most like to raise and explore?

EXERCISES AND ACTIVITIES FOR PSYCHODRAMA

Rationale

Psychodrama is based on the rationale that therapeutic work is enhanced by dealing with problems as though they are occurring in the present. The following exercises, activities, and problems are designed to give you some experience with psychodrama; experiment with them as much as possible in your group. These exercises will help you directly experience your concerns, release feelings, and gain insight. They will also help you increase your awareness of others' experiences and thus help you to develop more sensitivity to others.

As you work through these activities in small groups, think of imaginative ways to modify them.

Exercises

1. You are setting up a psychodrama for your group. What warm-up techniques would you use? Practice these techniques in your group and get feedback on your effectiveness from fellow group members.

2. You encourage a member of the group you are leading to role play a situation involving a conflict with her father. She says "I won't role play, because that seems phony. Role playing always makes me self-conscious. Is it okay if I just talk about my problem with my father instead?" How would you respond? (You might act this out in your own class group; have one person role play the reluctant member and another person the leader. Group members should take turns playing the roles so that several ways of working with reluctance can be demonstrated.)

3. As a group leader, how would you encourage members to select significant personal issues to explore in a psychodrama without coercing them to participate?

4. Assume that a member tells you that he'd like to get involved in a particular psychodrama because he has a lot of anger stored up against women. He tells you, however, that he is afraid that, if he does get involved, he will lose control and perhaps even make the women in the group the target of his rage. He is afraid he might "go crazy" if he takes the lid off his feelings. How would you respond?

5. A man in your group wants to explore his relationship with his daughter, which he describes as being strained. How would you proceed with him? What specific techniques might you suggest? What would you expect to accomplish with these procedures?

6. One of the women in the group describes her conflicts with her daughter as follows: "My daughter tells me that I simply don't understand what it's like to be 16. We fight continually, and the more I try to get her to do what I think is right, the more defiant she becomes. I simply don't know where to begin. How can I reach her?"

   Act out the above situation in your class or small group. Assume you are the leader and get another person in class to role play the mother. Consider trying these techniques:

- Role reversal (mother becomes the daughter)

- Self-presentation (mother presents her side of this conflict)

- Presentation of the other (mother presents the daughter's side)

- Soliloquy (mother verbalizes uncensored feelings/thoughts)

What other techniques can you think of to practice in this situation?

7. Assume that the woman in the above case is role playing with another member, who is playing the daughter. All of a sudden the mother stops and says "I'm stuck; I just don't know what to say now. Whenever she gets that hurt look in her eyes and begins to cry I feel rotten, guilty, and I freeze up. What can I do now?"

   In this instance, try the double technique (another member becomes an auxiliary ego and stands behind the mother and speaks for her). You could also use the multiple double technique (where two or more people represent different facets of the mother). One double might represent the guilty mother who attempts to placate her daughter, while the other double could be the firm mother who deals directly with the daughter's manipulation.

8. One of the women in your group seems aloof and judgmental. Members in the group pick up nonverbal cues such as frowning, certain glances and positioning of her head, and other indications of superiority. She says that people outside of the group have the same impression of her, yet she does not feel judgmental, nor does she perceive herself as others do.

   Assume that this woman wants to explore this issue and use the mirror technique. Someone in your class group can play the role of the woman who is perceived as aloof and judgmental, and you or another member can imitate her posture, gestures, and speech. Can you think of other techniques to help this woman explore the discrepancy between her self-image and the view others have of her?

9. Think of a situation where the use of the magic shop technique would be appropriate. Think of another case where you'd be likely to employ the future projection technique. If possible, set up these situations in your class/group and get practice using these techniques.

10. Select a personal problem that you are presently concerned about or a relationship that you'd like to understand better. (You must be willing to share this problem in your class/group. If dealing with a current problem seems too threatening, consider working on a past problem that you have resolved.) Then set up a psychodrama in your group in which you are the protagonist. This exercise, if done properly, will give you a sense of what it's like to be a member of a psychodrama group.

QUESTIONS FOR DISCUSSION AND EVALUATION

1. What problems, if any, would you predict for yourself as a participant in a psychodrama? What about being a leader/director of one?

2. What are the advantages of the action-oriented methods of psychodrama in which members actually act out and experience their conflicts as opposed to merely talking about them? What limitations or disadvantages do you see in this approach?

3. Psychodrama consists of verbally and nonverbally releasing pent-up feelings such as anger, hatred, despair, and so on. Do you feel able to deal with the release of your intense feelings? Have you already experienced a similar type of catharsis? Do you think that you have the knowledge and the skills to effectively deal with people who express such intense emotions? Could you deal with the emotional effects it may trigger in other group members?

4. How can cognitive work be incorporated into the emotional aspects of psychodrama? In your view, if a leader discontinues the helping process after people have expressed pent-up emotions, is this enough to lead to insight and behavioral change? How might you assist people to progress by thinking about what they've experienced and putting it into a cognitive framework so that meaning can be added to experience?

5. With what kind of clients do you think psychodrama would be most appropriate and effective? Are there certain populations for whom the method would be contra-indicated?

6. What are some specific psychodrama techniques that you'd want to incorporate into your style of leadership?

7. Do you see any limitations to using psychodrama as an exclusive method in a group, without combining it with the concepts and techniques of other approaches?

8. What do you think are the main values and contributions of psychodrama?

9. What are some possible psychological risks associated with psychodrama? How would you caution group members before they participated in a psychodrama? How do you think the potential dangers can be reduced?

10. If you were using psychodrama, what steps would you take to see that members were not left hanging with unfinished business? What would you do if a group member were left very open to intense emotions at the end of a group meeting?

8

The Existential-Humanistic Approach

PRECHAPTER PRIMER AND SELF-INVENTORY FOR
THE EXISTENTIAL-HUMANISTIC APPROACH TO GROUPS

Directions: Refer to page 34 for general directions. Indicate your position
on each statement, using the following code:

5 = I strongly agree with this statement.

4 = I agree, in most respects, with this statement.

3 = I am undecided in my opinion about this statement.

2 = I disagree, in most respects, with this statement.

1 = I strongly disagree with this statement.

_____ 1. Group work should focus on the subjective aspects of a member's
experience.

_____ 2. The central issues in counseling and therapy are freedom, responsibility, and the anxiety that accompanies being both free and responsible.

_____ 3. Anxiety and guilt are not necessarily disorders to be cured, for
these are a part of the human condition.

_____ 4. Being aware of death gives meaning to life and makes each person
realize that he or she is ultimately alone.

_____ 5. Group therapy's basic task is to expand consciousness and thus ex-
tend freedom.

STAGES OF DEVELOPMENT OF THE EXISTENTIAL-HUMANISTIC GROUP

Dimension	Initial Stage	Working Stage	Final Stage
Key developmental tasks and goals	The focus is on how members perceive and experience their world; thus the approach is experiential and subjective. The main goal is to increase awareness of options in order to widen everyone's brackets of freedom. The initial task of a group is to make a commitment to explore personally meaningful and significant issues concerning human struggles.	Members explore a wide range of universal human concerns such as loneliness, the anxiety of recognizing that one is free to make choices and that freedom always is accompanied by responsibility, the meaning of life, death, and so on. Participants consider alternative ways of dealing with issues they are facing in life. Emphasis is on taking responsibility _now_ for the way one chooses to be. Focus is on self-discovery, which often leads to giving up defenses and living authentically.	Group counseling or therapy is seen as an "invitation to change." Members are challenged to re-create themselves. In group, they have opportunities to evaluate their lives and to make choices as to how they will change. Toward the end of a group, termination is another issue to face, for the ending of a group brings on anxiety. "Death" of a group must be dealt with fully.
Role of group leader and tasks	Leader's tasks are to confront members with the issue of dealing with freedom and responsibility and to challenge members to recognize that, regardless of the limits of choosing, there is always some element of choice in life.	Emphasis is on creating an "I-Thou" relationship, which entails the leader's full presence. Leader's task is to be there as a person for the members; he or she embarks on an unknown journey with the members and is open to where they will go together. Leaders must understand and adopt the members' subjective worlds. Leaders also engage in self-disclosure and model authentic behavior.	At the final stage of a group, leader challenges the members to go into the world and be active. Leader helps the members to integrate and to consolidate what they've learned in the group so that the maximum transfer can occur. Rather than "doing therapy," leader lives _it_ through the openness of ongoing existential encounters with the members in the group.
Role of group members	Members always have a part in the group process. They look at _who_ and what they are; they clarify their identities and make decisions concerning how they can achieve authenticity. Members decide what they will explore in the group.	Members decide what struggles or existential concerns they will share. Typical concerns include changing roles, creating new identities when old identities are no longer meaningful, value conflicts, emptiness, dealing with loneliness, and working on the fear of freedom and responsibility.	In order to change, members must go out into the world and _act_. Since members are responsible for their own lives, they decide if and how they want to live differently. If a group is successful, members achieve authentic identities, become aware of choices that can lead to action.

56

Techniques	There are no prescribed techniques, and therapeutic procedures can be borrowed from many approaches. More than a group leader's technique or skill, the leader's attitude and behavior are crucial for the group's results. Group leaders are not viewed as technical experts who apply therapeutic treatment plans. There is no assessment, nor is there a predetermined treatment plan for the group to follow.	Emphasis is not so much on doing therapy by using techniques, rather it is on creating an "I-Thou" relationship and being fully present. Thus, leaders may work with dreams, they may work with the current interaction in the group, they may explore the past with members, and they may be both supportive and challenging. Emphasis is on constructive confrontation so that members can learn how to confront themselves.	Since group counseling or therapy is seen as a spontaneous encounter between members (and between members and the leader), the leader is free to draw on a diverse range of techniques from many other therapies. Although the focus is on the encounter that occurs in the group, specific techniques can be developed to challenge the members to recognize the choices they have and the decisions to make a new life.

Reactions: Summarize your reactions to the existential-humanistic perspective on group developmental stages. What do you like most? Least? What aspects of this approach would you incorporate into your style of leadership?

Questions: What questions about existential-humanistic therapy would you most like to raise and explore?

_____ 6. The meaning of death should be examined in group therapy sessions.

_____ 7. The group leader's function is not to tell members what life should mean to them but to encourage them to discover this meaning for themselves.

_____ 8. An inauthentic existence consists of living a life as outlined and determined by others, rather than a life based on one's own inner experience.

_____ 9. The effective counselor is less concerned with "doing therapy" than he or she is in living therapy by being with another.

_____ 10. Therapists' major tasks are fostering self-disclosure, creating "I-thou" relationships, and providing a model for clients.

SUMMARY OF THE BASIC ASSUMPTIONS AND KEY CONCEPTS
OF THE EXISTENTIAL-HUMANISTIC APPROACH TO GROUPS

1. The therapist focuses on independent choice and freedom, the potential within humans to find their own way, and the search for identity and self-actualization.

2. People become what they choose to become, and, although there are factors that restrict choices, ultimately self-determination is the basis of their uniqueness as individuals.

3. Group-therapy work should emphasize such themes as meaning in life, guilt, anxiety, responsibility, death, and one's ultimate aloneness.

4. The therapist's ultimate goal is to enable clients to be free and responsible for the direction of their own lives. Therefore, the clients are largely responsible for what occurs in therapy.

5. The therapist's major tasks are to grasp the subjective worlds of their clients and to establish authentic relationships in which clients can work on understanding themselves and their choices more fully.

6. Group leaders do not behave in rigid or prescribed ways, for they can't predict the exact direction or content of any group. Leaders are not technical experts who carry out treatment plans with specialized techniques, rather they establish real relationships with the members of the group.

7. The presence of the leader, or the leader's willingness to be there for others and confront them when appropriate, is a major characteristic of the effective group. Group leaders must be willing to take responsibility for their own thinking, feeling, and judging. They are present as persons with the members, for they become active agents in the group.

8. Existential-humanistic theory does not aim at "curing sick people," because it holds that it isn't possible to "cure" or to "remove" certain basic human conditions. Existential crises are seen as a part of living

and not something to be remedied. These crises frequently concern the meaning of life, anxiety and guilt, and the fear of choosing and accepting responsibility for one's choices. Because these "crises" aren't necessarily pathological, they can't be externally alleviated; they should be lived through and understood in the context of a group.

EXERCISES AND ACTIVITIES FOR THE
EXISTENTIAL-HUMANISTIC APPROACH TO GROUPS

Rationale

The existential-humanistic approach does not provide a ready-made set of techniques for group practitioners. It is more of an orientation to group counseling than a system of therapeutic procedures. Practitioners can adhere to the existential-humanistic perspective and at the same time use many of the other therapeutic techniques.

What follows are examples of activities that are in some way related to existential-humanistic themes. Use these exercises both on your own and in your group/class, and then you'll have a better idea how to integrate existential-humanistic counseling concepts into your leadership style. Think about what you can learn about both yourself and group processes through these exercises.

Exercises

1. Self-awareness. Group members often claim that they are afraid of learning too much about themselves. They may accept the notion that "ignorance is bliss" or "what they don't know won't hurt them." What is your position on this? Are you clearly open to learning all that you can about yourself? Or, do you have reservations about expanding your self-awareness? What concerns might you have about opening doors to your life that are now closed? Discuss these questions in your class/group.

2. Freedom and responsibility. Freedom of choice entails accepting the responsibility for influencing the direction of your life. Being free means that, as long as you are alive, you are making choices about who you are becoming. Do you believe that you are what you are now largely as a result of your choices, or do you feel that you are the product of circumstances? What are some major choices that you've made that have been crucial to your present development? Discuss some of these crucial decisions in your group. How do you imagine your life would be different now if you had decided differently.

3. Anxiety. Anxiety is not only an impetus to change, it is also a result of recognizing that you are responsible for your choices. What kind of anxiety have you experienced in terms of making key life decisions? How do you tend to manage your anxiety: By directly facing the consequences of your choices? By attempting to make others responsible for you? By avoiding making choices? By attempting to deny reality? Do you agree with the existential notion that anxiety produces growth? How well do you manage anxiety in your own life? In what situations do you experience the most anxiety?

4. Death. How well are you able to accept the fact of your own death? Do you see any relationship between how you view death and the degree to which you are living fully now? In order to clarify your thoughts and feelings about death and to examine how death affects the way you live, try some of the following exercises in your class or group.

    a. What do you think the significant people in your life would write on your tombstone? What would you like them to say?

    b. Write the eulogy you'd like delivered at your funeral. Bring it to group and share it with other members.

    c. Assume that you knew you were going to die within 24 hours. What would you most like to do during these final hours? What does this say about your values?

    d. Tell others in your group what you'd most like to accomplish before you die.

    e. If you have experienced the loss of someone close to you, consider sharing what this has been like for you. What did you learn about yourself through this experience?

5. Meaning in life. Confronting our mortality makes us think about how meaningful our lives are. In your group, let yourself imagine a typical day in your life five years ago. What was it like and what were you like then? Are there any major differences between your life then and now? Share some of the most significant changes you've made over the past five years with others in your group. Then, project yourself into the future five years from now. What do you hope you'll be like then? What do you fear you might be like then? Explore in your group what you are experiencing currently in your life that contributes to or detracts from a meaningful existence.

6. Authenticity. The existential-humanistic perspective stresses that affirming ourselves and discovering who we are are ongoing processes. We are authentic if we face the anxiety of choosing for ourselves and accept the consequences of our choices. Inauthentic people allow others to determine who and what they are. Discuss some crucial incidents in your own personal struggles to define yourself. Consider some of these questions as you construct your personal-identity road map:

    • Who am I? What has contributed to the way I am?

    • What roles have I typically played? How have I seen myself?

    • What choices did I make? What choices did others make for me?

    • Have I lost contact with myself by looking to others for answers and direction? Do I trust others more than myself?

    • How has my life been shaped by past actions, people, influences, and so on?

- What more do I want from my life? What kind of identity am I searching for?

- If some of the elements that I depend on for a sense of my identity were taken away, what would I be like?

7. Loneliness. Share in your group some ways that each of you has experienced loneliness. Can you recall the time in your life when you felt most alone? What was this like for you? Select a poem, a picture, or an excerpt from a book that captures the loneliness you have felt at some time in your life. Bring this to group and share it.

8. Creative solitude. Existential-humanists believe that, unless we can enjoy solitude creatively, we cannot develop genuine intimacy with others. Do you make time for yourself to be alone? When you are alone, what is this generally like for you? Do you welcome it or flee from it? Select a song, poem, poster, or picture that represents peaceful solitude to you. In what ways might you want to learn how to enjoy time alone?

9. Role and functions of the group leader. The existential-humanistic approach emphasizes the role of the leader not so much as a doer of therapy but as a person to be fully present with the group members. Discuss in your group the degree to which you feel personally equipped to challenge others to look at the important issues in life. For instance, do you feel ready to challenge others to look at the choices they've made as well as the ones now open to them? Have you done this in your own live? Could you be psychologically with another person who was exploring a life/death issue? Have you been willing to face such issues in your life?

10. Personal evaluation and critique. In your group or class, explore the concepts of the existential-humanistic approach you find most valuable. What would you borrow from this approach? What are the limitations of the approach? What disadvantages do you see in limiting yourself strictly to an existential-humanistic orientation? Do you think this perspective has something to offer every client? For what kinds of people do you think it is the most appropriate? How are you able to relate in a personal way to the existential-humanistic approach? What are the therapeutic techniques from other models that you'd use to apply existential-humanistic concepts in the groups you lead or will lead?

CHAPTER
9
The Person-Centered Approach

PRECHAPTER PRIMER AND SELF-INVENTORY FOR THE
PERSON-CENTERED APPROACH TO GROUPS

Directions: Refer to page 34 for general directions. Indicate your position
on each statement, using the following code:

    5 = I strongly agree with this statement.

    4 = I agree, in most respects, with this statement.

    3 = I am undecided in my opinion about this statement.

    2 = I disagree, in most respects, with this statement.

    1 = I strongly disagree with this statement.

_____ 1. The group members, not the leader, have the primary responsibility
          for the direction the group takes.

_____ 2. The attitudes of acceptance, empathy, warmth, respect, genuineness,
          and positive regard are both necessary and sufficient for therapeu-
          tic change to occur.

_____ 3. A leader's direction is not necessary for a group to move in a con-
          structive direction.

_____ 4. A major function of the group leader is to establish a climate of
          trust in the group.

_____ 5. A group leader can be effective without attending to transference.

_____ 6. Self-disclosure on the leader's part tends to increase trust and self-disclosure on the part of the members.

_____ 7. Group members should be involved in choosing the techniques or structured exercises used in the group.

_____ 8. The group leader is more of a facilitator than a director.

_____ 9. Directive intervention by the leader can interfere with the group process.

_____ 10. Group leaders should avoid giving advice.

SUMMARY OF THE BASIC ASSUMPTIONS AND KEY CONCEPTS OF THE PERSON-CENTERED APPROACH TO GROUPS

1. Clients are basically trustworthy and have the potential for self-direction. The group can become aware of problems and the means to resolve them if the group facilitator encourages them to explore present feelings and thoughts.

2. Because the group has the potential for self-direction, there is a minimum of direction on the leader's part, for this tends to undermine respect for the group members.

3. External measures such as diagnosis, testing, interpretation, advice giving, and probing for information are not used. Instead, therapy comprises active listening, reflection and clarification, and understanding the inner world of the client.

4. The therapeutic relationship between group leader and members helps the members grow and change. The therapist must reflect warmth, acceptance, respect, caring, empathy, and must not be judgmental.

QUESTIONS FOR DISCUSSION AND EVALUATION

1. <u>Group goals</u>. Do you agree with Rogers' contention that the group has the capacity to move in constructive directions without structure, direction, and active intervention on the leader's part? Why or why not? What are the implications for practice if you accept this assumption? Do you agree that group members are the ones to formulate <u>specific</u> goals?

2. <u>Attending and listening</u>. How well do you listen and attend? What gets in your way of fully attending to others? How can you improve your attending skills?

3. <u>Empathy</u>. What is your understanding of empathy? How can you become empathic? What are the barriers to this? Do you expect to have the problem of overidentification—losing your own identity by immersing yourself in another's world? What part does leader self-disclosure play in advanced levels of empathy? How can you improve your ability to develop appropriate empathy for others?

STAGES OF DEVELOPMENT OF THE PERSON-CENTERED GROUP

Dimension	Initial Stage	Working Stage	Final Stage
Key developmental tasks and goals	The early stages of group are characterized by some floundering and a search for direction. Typically, members present a socially acceptable facade or they reveal the "safer" sides of themselves; they describe themselves in a "there-and-then" manner. There is a milling around and a sense of confusion concerning the purpose and the function of the group. A key task is to build trust.	Negative feelings often surface over the lack of leadership. Then, a more accepting and trusting climate may prevail. Members show more of themselves, cohesion develops, and members find support in the group. Some confrontation occurs, especially when members sense that others are not being genuine. False fronts give way to a real expression of self.	The group develops a healing capacity, and members are able to move forward based on the support offered. Members develop self-acceptance; they offer feedback to each other in a climate of honesty and a sense of community develops. Behavior changes are noticed in the group. Members show increased ease in expressing their feelings and they gain insight into how they relate to others.
Role of group leader and tasks	The facilitator's main role is to grant freedom to the members to develop a structure of their own. The leader places responsibility on the group for the direction they will take. Group leaders have the job of being sensitive to whatever direction is taken by the group and follow that lead. Leader is concerned with creating a climate that is psychologically safe for the members. Leader's role is to be without a role. The central function is to help members interact honestly.	A central task of the leader is to adopt an empathic viewpoint; it is important that members feel deeply understood and cared for. Leader needs to accept negative as well as positive feelings. Leader needs to share own ongoing feelings and reactions with the group. Leader listens actively, reflects, clarifies, summarizes, links members' statements, demonstrates respect, and also shows acceptance and caring for the members.	The central role of the leader is to help members express how they have experienced this group and to encourage honest feedback. Leader should help members apply what they have learned in the group to life outside of it.
Role of group members	Members are expected to develop their own goals and decide for themselves how they will spend their time together. At first members are rather confused and they search for a structure. They are resistant to sharing personally significant material.	Members make the decision of what they will reveal about themselves; they express feelings to others in the group. They offer both support and challenge to others; they give and receive feedback. Members at this stage usually are willing to express immediate interpersonal feelings of both a positive and a negative nature. Self-exploration occurs on a deeper level.	Members move from playing roles to being real, from being relatively closed to being open and able to tolerate some ambiguity, from being out of contact with internal and subjective experience to being aware of the ongoing subjective process, from looking for external answers to looking inward for direction.

64

Techniques	Person-centered leaders tend to avoid using planned exercises and techniques to "get a group moving." They rely on the capacity of the group to decide how time will be spent. The leader's attitudes and personal characteristics are far more important than the techniques that are used.	Key techniques include active listening, reflection, clarification, self-disclosure, showing respect, congruence, and continuing to create a climate of trust. Members are encouraged to speak in an open way about whatever they are feeling at the moment. These do not represent techniques as much as basic attitudes/behaviors of the leader.	The group leader is really not necessary at this stage if the leader has been effective, for now the group is fairly self-directive and can draw on its own resources for direction. Leader may help the group members summarize what they have learned and encourage them to apply it to life outside the group.

Reactions: Summarize your reactions to the person-centered perspective on group developmental stages. What do you like most? Least? What aspects of this approach would you incorporate into your style of leadership?

Questions: What questions about person-centered therapy would you most like to raise and explore?

4. <u>Unconditional positive regard and acceptance</u>. What do the terms <u>unconditional positive regard</u> and <u>acceptance</u> mean to you? Rogers sees these as necessary qualities for therapeutic progress. Do you have these qualities? What might be some prejudices or assumptions you have that make it difficult for you to accept some people? Do you think that unconditional acceptance is desirable? Would you put certain conditions on your acceptance of people? If so, what might be some of these conditions?

5. <u>Respect</u>. What are some specific ways to demonstrate respect for group members? Do you think it's possible to work effectively with group members if you don't respect them? Why or why not? What are some common ways that group leaders can show disrespect to members?

6. <u>Genuineness</u>. What criteria can you employ to determine your level of genuineness? Rogers contends that genuineness is essential for a therapeutic relationship to develop. Do you agree? Is it possible to be an effective group leader and not be genuine? What problems do you predict you might have in "being yourself" as a group leader?

7. <u>Immediacy</u>. Direct mutual talk conveys immediacy. Leaders can model this direct form of communication for members. What might get in your way of being direct? When is immediacy especially useful in a group?

8. <u>Concreteness</u>. Group members and leaders often speak in vague and general terms. How can you become more concrete in your own responses? How can you assist members to become more concrete in the ways they express their thoughts and feelings?

9. <u>Confrontation</u>. What is confrontation as you see it? Does it occupy a central place in person-centered therapy? How can confrontation be combined with support? How can you challenge members without causing them to become increasingly defensive? What are your guidelines for using confrontation as a leader? What problems might you have that could make it difficult for you to confront members, even when it is needed?

10. <u>Role and functions of the group leader</u>. According to the person-centered view, the counselor in a group is more of a <u>facilitator</u> than a director, leader, teacher, or trainer. As a facilitator, your job is to create a psychological climate of safety and acceptance, which supposedly allows the members to use their own resources constructively. What do you think of this role? Could you function effectively in such a role? Why or why not?

11. <u>Evaluation and research</u>. Rogers stresses subjective research on group process and outcomes, consisting mainly of self-reports by the participants. What are your ideas concerning subjective measures to determine the outcomes of a group? What are some of your ideas regarding ways of finding out whether or not a group is successful? How would you evaluate the outcome of your groups?

12. <u>Critique of person-centered approach</u>. Give your personal evaluation and critique of this model, using some of these questions as a guide:

• What would it be like for you to lead a group with a strict person-centered orientation?

• Do you think that techniques, knowledge of theory, and leadership skills are <u>less</u> important than the attitude of the counselor? Why or why not?

• Can you use many of the concepts and attitudes of this approach as a foundation for creating a therapeutic relationship and thus as a springboard to using other therapeutic technqiues? If so, how?

• What are your major criticisms of this model?

• What are the major contributions of the person-centered model to group therapy?

CHAPTER
10

Gestalt Therapy

PRECHAPTER PRIMER AND SELF-INVENTORY FOR
GESTALT GROUP THERAPY

<u>Directions</u>: Refer to page 34 for general directions. Indicate your position
on each statement, using the following code:

5 = I <u>strongly agree</u> with this statement.

4 = I <u>agree</u>, in most respects, with this statement.

3 = I am <u>undecided</u> in my opinion about this statement.

2 = I <u>disagree</u>, in most respects, with this statement.

1 = I <u>strongly disagree</u> with this statement.

_____ 1. The goal of group counseling is to help each group member integrate
the fragmented parts of his or her personality to the extent that
each person can carry on the process of development alone.

_____ 2. Group work should focus on here-and-now experiencing in order to
increase members' awareness.

_____ 3. Past conflicts or events are best understood by re-experiencing
them in the here-and-now.

_____ 4. It is generally more productive to ask "what" and "how" questions
than to ask "why" questions.

_____ 5. Unfinished business from the past tends to manifest itself in one's current behavior.

_____ 6. Group work should focus on the members' present feelings, experiencing, awareness, nonverbal messages, and blocks to awareness.

_____ 7. Fantasy is a potentially powerful therapeutic tool.

_____ 8. It is important to focus on both verbal and nonverbal language as group work proceeds.

_____ 9. The best way to deal with future concerns is to bring them into the here-and-now.

_____ 10. Interpretation of group members' dreams is one of the leader's major methods of increasing group members' awareness.

SUMMARY OF THE BASIC ASSUMPTIONS AND KEY CONCEPTS OF THE GESTALT-THERAPY APPROACH TO GROUPS

1. The here-and-now of the group members' experience is most important. The group leader focuses on _what_ and _how_, instead of _why_, and on anything that prevents effective functioning in the present.

2. People are personally responsible for what they feel.

3. Unfinished business from the past can interfere with effective functioning in the here-and-now. In order to remove this interference, group members should be encouraged to re-experience this business in the present.

4. Rather than resolving polarities and splits within them, people should simply recognize and accept these polarities.

5. The therapist should challenge group members to see how they are avoiding responsibility for their own feelings and encourage them to look for internal, rather than external, support.

6. Gestalt therapists use a wide range of action-oriented techniques in assisting group members to increase their awareness. Through group interaction, it is assumed that members will become more aware of conflicts and places where they "get stuck" (arrive at an impasse), and, in the group, they can experiment with a variety of techniques to work through the impasse and move to a new level of integration.

STAGES OF DEVELOPMENT OF THE GESTALT GROUP

Dimensions	Initial Stage	Working Stage	Final Stage
Key developmental tasks and goals	A central goal is to gain here-and-now awareness of what is being felt, sensed, and thought; group members must experiment and experience.	In the working stage of a group, the members deal with unfinished business from the past that is impeding full functioning now. The task is to integrate polarities. Group therapy is aimed at helping members to give expression to the side of themselves that they tend to repress.	Members assume personal responsibility, which means that they integrate the fragmented aspects of their personalities. By achieving a moment-to-moment awareness of whatever is being experienced, members have within themselves the means to make changes.
Role of group leader and tasks	It is the leader's task to follow whatever leads are provided by the group members; in this way, the members are able to become aware of the what and the how of their experiencing.	The leader's task is to pay close attention to both the verbal and the nonverbal messages of members and to go with what is obvious. By focusing on the obvious, therapy becomes meaningful. The leader suggests experiments designed to enhance and intensify the experience of the members.	After a piece of work is completed the leader may ask members to state how they are feeling. There is not much emphasis on cognitive structuring or behavior modification assignments. It is assumed that, once members gain an awareness of what they are doing to prevent themselves from fully experiencing the moment, they are capable of changing.
Role of group members	Members are expected to focus on the here-and-now and to re-experience past conflicts as though they were going on now. The members decide what they will explore in the group.	Members are expected to directly communicate to one another and to make "I" statements. They are discouraged from asking "why" questions and instead are urged to make personal statements. The focus is on exploration of feelings. To experience these feelings fully, members take part in a variety of action-oriented activities. They don't talk about problems, rather they are asked to act out their various roles and conflicts.	Members give and receive feedback. Members have the opportunity to identify unfinished business from their pasts that impedes present functioning and to work through impasses. By gaining awareness of areas that were out-of-awareness, they become more integrated. They are increasingly able to live with their own polarities.

70

Techniques	The leader uses what and how questions, but not why questions, to help members focus on themselves and what they might be experiencing. Leaders may use many techniques, such as fantasy approaches, asking people to pay attention to what they are experiencing physically, thinking out loud, and so on.	A wide range of experiential techniques all have the general goal of helping the members to intensify their experiencing in the present moment. Members may explore dreams by becoming all parts of their dreams, or they may engage in role playing in which they act out all the parts or they may exaggerate a particular gesture or mannerism. Symbolic encounters are used to help members deal with unfinished situations.	Members can be asked to enact a situation the way they'd like it to be, only they play all the parts. Members are often asked to put a new ending to an old and unfinished situation. Techniques help members see how past unfinished situations get in the way of effective living in the present.

Reactions: Summarize your reactions to the Gestalt perspective on group developmental stages. What do you like most? Least? What aspects of this approach would you incorporate into your style of leadership?

Questions: What questions about Gestalt therapy would you most like to raise and explore?

71

EXERCISES AND ACTIVITIES FOR GESTALT GROUPS

Rationale

Gestalt therapy makes use of a variety of action-oriented techniques that are designed to intensify what members are presently experiencing. Instead of discussing conflicts, for example, members in the Gestalt group are encouraged to "become the conflict." The idea is to fully experience every dimension of ourselves (be authentic). The Gestaltist contends that, when we get close to feelings that make us uncomfortable, we tend to avoid these feelings and thus do not really fully experience the various dimensions of a conflict. The Gestalt therapist will suggest experiments to members that will help them try some new behavior and thus will assist group members to experience everything fully.

It is important that the following exercises not be done mechanically. Each exercise is best tailored to the unique needs of the members in your class/group. Further, it is a good idea to give members some preparation before springing an experiment on them. Enlist the cooperation of group members by giving brief explanations of the basic purpose of each exercise. By trying many of the following exercises in your own small group, you will be in a better position to know which of these techniques you might want to use when you are a group leader.

Exercises

1. Here-and-Now versus There-and-Then. Talk about a personal experience in the past tense for about three minutes. Now, take the same experience, only this time relive the experience as though it were happening now. What difference do you notice between these 3-minute exercises? What value do you see in encouraging people in groups to make past experiences into present-centered ones?

2. Bringing the future into the now. Are you anticipating any future confrontations? This exercise can be a form of rehearsal. Using the two-chair technique, be yourself, then become the person you expect to confront, then be yourself, and so on. Make this future event happen in the here-and-now. Do so briefly. When you are finished, discuss what this was like. What did you learn through the experiment? What are your fears and hopes regarding this future event?

3. How do you accept and avoid personal responsibility? Using a go-around approach, subgroups, or dyads, have each member say how he or she avoids accepting responsibility for his or her own thoughts, actions, feelings, and moods. How can you begin to accept more of the responsibility for the ways you blame others for your emotional states: Examples—"You make me mad." "You get me jealous." "You keep me from doing what I really want to do."

4. Identifying unfinished business. Gestalt therapy emphasizes the role of old business that hangs around and gets in the way of our being effective and alive now. In your group, without discussing them, mention one or two areas or specific examples of unfinished business. Then, you might add

how you could work toward dealing with these unfinished themes. Some examples of unfinished business are:

- feeling stuck with guilt;

- feeling resentful, and not expressing the resentment;

- experiencing grief that has not been fully expressed.

5. Avoidance. The concept of avoidance is central in Gestalt therapy. How many ways can you think of that you avoid things? Do you reach an impasse because you are afraid of feeling uncomfortable? Do you avoid giving up games because you are afraid of what life would be like without them? Do you avoid changing by convincing yourself that you cannot change? Do you avoid by trying to convince yourself that you are perfectly satisfied? Do you avoid by blaming others? Try living out some of these avoidance techniques in your group. For example, really blame others for your inability to change.

6. Language approaches. In order to see how language can be used to alienate ourselves from ourselves as well as others, deliberately try to use language as impersonally as you can. Conduct a short conversation using language that keeps you from being responsible for yourself and that is designed to alienate others. Here are some guidelines to a distant and impersonal language style:

- Say it instead of I.

- Use you when you are really talking about yourself.

- Talk about yourself (be sure to say you) and avoid making I statements.

- Ask questions. Try pelleting others with questions for a few moments—interrogate, ask a lot of why questions, and take care to keep yourself out of any interchange.

- Use plenty of qualifiers; that is, either before you say anything or at the end of any sentence, use a qualifier or a disclaimer such as, but, maybe, sort of, kind of, perhaps, possibly, I guess, I suppose, and so on.

- Say can't a lot (even if you know you can); saying can't will cement your feelings of helplessness.

- Pepper your talk with a good dose of shoulds and oughts. Be sure to tell others what they should do, how they should feel, what they should think; and tell them how they ought to be and ought not to be.

Talk about how it feels to talk this way, and get feedback from the group on how they experienced you doing this.

7. Nonverbal language in group. Exaggerate some of your typical body language. If you often frown, let yourself really get into that frown. If

you have a certain mannerism, develop it fully. What can you learn from this exercise about your nonverbal language?

Pay attention to others as they speak for a time and note the tone of voice, the manner of speech, the quality of voice, the posture, facial expressions, gestures, the speed and rate of speech, and so on. What do people tell you about themselves nonverbally?

Finally, each person in your group might try "becoming" one aspect of his or her body language. For example, Marilyn could "become" her tight mouth and then speak "for" her mouth—"I am my tightness, I'm holding my words back from you. I'm not going to be open, and if you want something from me you'll have to pry me open."

8. <u>Experimenting with dialogues</u>. Each person in the group at some time might want to experiment with the dialogue game. You can also do this at home alone. Simply get two chairs and put them facing each other. Next, choose one of your conflicts; become one side of this conflict and talk to the other side, which is in the other chair. Get up and sit in the other chair and now become that other side. Carry on this dialogue for a time. If you're doing this in group, discuss what you learned from the dialogue after you've finished. What was it like for you to do the experiment? What side felt dominant? Here are some examples of typical conflicts that often keep us fragmented:

• Part of me wants to open up, the other part of me wants to keep closed.

• There is the serious side of me, and then there is the fun side.

• I want to love, yet I don't dare let myself.

• Part of me wants to risk, the other part wants to play it safe.

List as many types of conflicts/fragmentations that exist inside of you as you can. Do you have trouble integrating dichotomies such as: tough/tender; masculine/feminine; worthwhile/worthless?

9. <u>Fantasy approaches</u>. Try some fantasy experiments in group. For instance, allow yourself to live out some of your expectations and fears. If you are afraid of being rejected, live out your rejection fantasies in your group. You can also use the rehearsal technique; as you think of your fantasy, repeat all your thoughts out loud.

10. <u>Gestalt dream work</u>. Try some Gestalt dream experiments in your group. For example, become all the parts of a dream—act them out in the present tense and let yourself really experience the dream. Or, carry on a dialogue between various parts of the dream. What does your dream teach you about yourself?

11. <u>Making the rounds</u>. In this exercise, a member goes around to everyone in the group and says something to each person—usually something that he or she is attempting to deny, something that is difficult to say, or something that he or she typically does not express. Make up some incomplete sentences, and experiment with making the rounds and completing these sentences. Some examples of incomplete sentences are:

- "If I were to depend on you, then _____."

- "I keep my distance from you by _____."

- "If I were to get close to you, then _____."

- "If I'm not always in control _____."

- "One way I'd try to control you is _____."

- "If I would not smile when I'm in pain I _____."

- "When I look at you _____."

Any of these sentences can be selected and completed for every person in the room. It is important that, in doing this exercise, you respond quickly and give your uncensored and initial reaction. After you've experienced a go-around it would be useful to talk about what you learned from it, what it was like for you to do this, and where you could go from here.

You can also experiment with making concise statements to each person in the group, using the go-around method. For example, if you find it difficult to ask for anything for yourself, you could go to each person and ask for something.

12. Rehearsal. Internal rehearsal saps much of our vitality. We often think carefully about the appropriate way to be, so that any spontaneity is squelched. The rehearsal technique consists of saying out loud what you are thinking silently. In this exercise, select a situation in which you would typically rehash all the pros and cons to yourself before deciding what to do or say—but this time allow yourself to think out loud. In your rehearsal, let yourself ham it up a bit and really get the feel of the exercise. For example, let yourself act out in group what you go through before you ask a person for a date. What are all the things you say to yourself? (The exercise can make you more acutely aware of how you are striving for approval or how much you fear rejection.)

13. Reversal techniques. In this procedure, you give expression to a side of yourself that rarely gets expressed. Gestalt theory posits that each person's polarities crave expression, yet are often not acknowledged much less directly expressed. For example, the very prim and proper lady in the group who continually worries about the appropriateness of her performances can be invited to experiment with deliberately inappropriate behavior. She is given permission to be unladylike. The rationale here is that integration of polarities is possible if you allow yourself to plunge into the very thing that produces anxiety in you.

14. The Secret. This exercise can be useful in exploring fears, guilt feelings, and catastrophic expectations. Think of a personal secret. Don't actually share the secret in group, but imagine yourself doing so. What do you imagine it would be like if others knew your secret? What are your fears? How do you imagine they'd respond? (If you'd like, you can discuss these fears or your fantasy experience in group.)

15. <u>The projection exercise</u>. At times, people accuse others of the very things that they refuse to see in themselves. For example, you may see others as being critical and judgmental of you, yet fail to experience the ways you may be very critical and judgmental of others. In this exercise, you make a direct statement to others in the group and then apply it to yourself. For instance, you might say to Al "You continually expect <u>me</u> to be more than I am in here." Then turn it around and say "Al, I expect more from you in this group." Try a new statement with each person and apply all of these sentences to yourself. What can you learn from this exercise?

16. Review all of the preceding exercises and decide what techniques you might use in working with the following conflicts:

   • trust versus mistrust

   • the desire to get close <u>and</u> the need to pull away

   • being weak versus being strong

   • the will to risk <u>and</u> the need to play it safe

   • being appropriate versus being inappropriate

   • love <u>and</u> hate

   • the wish to express anger <u>and</u> the fear of doing so

   • dependence versus independence

   • wanting to self-disclose <u>and</u> wanting to remain secretive

   Can you think of other conflicts or problems whose solutions might be aided by the use of the Gestalt-therapy techniques you have learned about in these excercises?

QUESTIONS FOR DISCUSSION AND EVALUATION

1. Gestalt therapy is an action-oriented approach, one that requires the group leader to be active and employ a variety of experiments designed to enable members to intensify their feelings. How comfortable are you in using such an approach? What is your opinion of the therapeutic value of these Gestalt experiments? How do you imagine you would respond to these techniques as a group member?

2. Techniques cannot be separated from the personality of the leader and the relationship he or she has with the group members. Do you see the danger of a group leader becoming a mere technician and keeping him- or herself hidden through the use of techniques. If you are practicing Gestalt therapy, how can you avoid merely employing one gimmick after another? Would you, as a leader, tend to use these techniques as a way to get power? Discuss the potential for abuse of power by the group leader.

3. How can a therapist combine the Gestalt approach with other approaches, such as psychodrama, TA, and rational-emotive therapy? What kind of integration do you see with other systems?

4. What are your major criticisms of the Gestalt approach? What are its limitations and shortcomings? What are its strong points?

11
Transactional Analysis

PRECHAPTER PRIMER AND SELF-INVENTORY FOR THE TA GROUP

<u>Directions</u>: Refer to page 34 for general directions. Indicate your position on these statements, using the following code:

5 = I <u>strongly agree</u> with this statement.

4 = I <u>agree</u>, in most respects, with this statement.

3 = I am <u>undecided</u> in my opinion about this statement.

2 = I <u>disagree</u>, in most respects, with this statement.

1 = I <u>strongly disagree</u> with this statement.

_____ 1. For healthy personality development, positive stroking (physical and emotional touching) is essential.

_____ 2. Group leaders should play the roles of teacher, trainer, and resource person.

_____ 3. Contracts are both basic and necessary for the group-counseling process to be therapeutic.

_____ 4. Group members should develop independence and not rely on the group leader for guidance.

_____ 5. Relationships between the group leader and members must be equal if the group's work is to be successful.

_____ 6. Group members should be taught how to explore the early decisions and parental injunctions that influence them now.

_____ 7. Group members shoud be taught to examine the decisions they made early in life and determine if these decisions are still appropriate.

_____ 8. Game-playing, by its very definition, prevents the development of genuine intimacy.

_____ 9. People tend to accept uncritically messages they recieved from their parents and from parental substitutes.

_____ 10. Contracts give direction to group sessions, they increase the responsibility of members to actively participate in group work, and they provide a basis for equal partnership between the members and the leader.

SUMMARY OF THE BASIC ASSUMPTIONS AND KEY CONCEPTS
OF THE TA APPROACH TO GROUPS

1. Early in life people make necessary decisions that may no longer be appropriate in later life.

2. In order to make new, appropriate decisions, group members are taught to recognize ego states, to understand how injunctions and messages they incorporated as children affect them now, and to identify life scripts that determine their actions.

3. TA, then, is largely a didactic and cognitive form of therapy, with the goal of liberating group members from the past and assisting them to redecide how they will live based on new awareness.

4. Group members can best achieve these goals by being _active_ in the group-therapy process, and thus TA group therapists stress the equality of the therapeutic relationship between group members and therapists.

5. To assure that members actively and responsibly participate in the group-therapy process, they contract for work on specific issues, and these contracts direct the course of the group.

6. TA concepts and techniques are particularly appropriate for group work. It is in a group context that people best learn how they interact with one another, how decisions made early in life still influence them, and how to become aware of the games they play and the scripts they live out.

STAGES IN THE DEVELOPMENT OF THE TA GROUP

Dimension	Initial Stage	Working Stage	Final Stage
Key developmental tasks and goals	Group therapy begins with a contract, one that is acceptable to both the member and the leader. Group work is guided by the contract. An early basic task is to teach members the basics of TA, including how to recognize ego states, transactions, games, injunctions, rackets, and the significance of early decisions.	At the working stage, the basic developmental task is that members recognize and work through impasses. Much work is done with re-experiencing early decisions and situations from childhood, with the aim of making new decisions that are more appropriate for the present. Early decisions are reviewed critically and members think about ways they want to be different.	The focus at this stage of the group is on actually making new decisions. The basic premise is that what was decided earlier can now be redecided. Members learn to thrive on positive strokes, and they recognize the power that they possess. Contracts may be renegotiated and new work may begin.
Role of group leader and tasks	Leaders begin to teach the members at this stage that they are responsible for how they act, think, and feel. Leaders provide structure for the group, teach the basic concepts of TA, and may use role-playing and fantasy methods to have members relive certain scenes. Leaders help the members identify and clarify goals and develop a contract that will specify the work to be done.	At this stage the group leader assists members to recognize early decisions they made from a Child ego state, and then, from this same Child ego state, the members are encouraged to make new and more appropriate decisions. Leaders draw on a variety of techniques to help members work through impasses.	At the final stage of a group, the leaders mainly assist members in making new decisions and life-oriented contracts; members are encouraged to accept responsibility for changing their own lives.
Role of group members	Members are expected to formulate clear contracts. They learn the ego states they function in, they recognize the injunctions they've accepted, and they see the importance of understanding and challenging early decisions.	Members learn about the injunction-decision-racket complex. They identify life scripts. Members work through early experiences both cognitively and affectively.	During the final stage, the members decide how they will change. They may use the group to practice new behaviors. Feedback and support are given.

80

| Techniques | Contracts are a basic tool. Imagery and fantasy techniques may be used. Role playing may be used to promote a here-and-now focus. | A wide range of cognitive and affective techniques are used, including structural analysis, transactional analysis, analysis of games, cognitive restructuring, empty chair, life-script questionnaire, desensitization. Techniques in TA groups are designed to help members feel more intensely and to think and conceptualize. | Homework assignments may be used as a way of helping the members to fulfill their contracts. Gestalt techniques may be incorporated into the TA group, as may techniques drawn from behavioral methods, psychodrama, and other action-oriented approaches. |

Reactions: Summarize your reactions to the TA perspective on group developmental stages. What do you like most? Least? What aspects of this approach would you incorporate into your style of leadership?

Questions: What questions about TA therapy would you most like to raise and explore?

EXERCISES AND ACTIVITIES FOR THE TA APPROACH TO GROUPS

Rationale

Not all of the following exercises deal with therapeutic procedures routinely used by all TA practitioners; however, they are designed to increase your awareness of matters such as: What ego state do you tend to function in? What kind of strokes do you typically receive? Which of the parental messages that you picked up early in life do you still live by? How do your decisions made early in life still influence you? What games prevent intimacy? What basis can provide for new decisions?

Many of these exercises are cognitively oriented and are geared to get you to think about your assumptions and your behavior. I encourage you to think of imaginative ways of developing your own exercises; for example, experiment with combining some of these cognitively oriented TA concepts with some of the emotion-oriented techniques of Gestalt therapy. Use these exercises in your own small groups, and discuss specific aspects of this approach that you think you could use in the groups you lead.

Exercises

1. The ego states: Parent, adult, child. TA teaches people in groups to recognize when they are operating in their Parent, Adult, and Child ego states. Each person in your group should choose an ego state and remain in it during a group exercise. Each person should think and speak from the chosen ego state. The purpose of this exercise is to help you become aware of how you might function as a Parent without knowing it. As a variation, you might try having two group members conduct a debate between two ego states.

2. Stroking. TA stresses the need for strokes, both physical and psychological ones. In your group, talk about the specific types of strokes that you need to sustain you. What strokes do you seek? How do you get the strokes you want? Are you able to accept positive stroking, or do you have a need to discount them and set yourself up for negative stroking? You could also experiment with asking your group members for the kind of strokes you want.

    Discuss the idea of conditional strokes in your group. Were you brought up to believe that you would get strokes when you behaved in the expected manner? How does this relate to the kinds of strokes you get in your group?

3. Injunctions. Injunctions are messages that we have been programmed to accept—that is, messages that we have knowingly and unknowingly incorporated into our life-styles. In this experiment, each group member "becomes" his or her parent and gives injunctions. Each person should adopt the tone of voice that he or she imagines the parent would have used. Get involved in the exercise and really tell people the way you think they should be and should live.

    As a second part of this exercise you might discuss a few of the following injunctions as they apply to you. What are some other messages that you heard as a child? Add these to the list. Which of these messages still influence you?

- Dont' be _____.

- You should always do what is expected.

- Don't feel/think/be who you are.

- Don't succeed/fail.

- Don't trust others.

- Be perfect—never make a mistake.

- Be more than you are.

- Don't be impulsive.

- Don't be sexy.

- Don't be aggressive.

- Keep your feelings to yourself.

- You ought to think of others before yourself.

- You should never have negative thoughts.

Which of these injunctions have you accepted uncritically? Which of them do you most want to modify?

4. Decisions and redecisions. In the TA group, there is a lot of emphasis on evaluating the present appropriateness of decisions made early in life. People tend to cling to early decisions and look for evidence to support these decisions. However, TA assumes that what has been decided can be redecided.

     In your group, devote some time to identifying decisions that you made early in life that you may still be living by. Then, after you identify these decisions, determine what you do to keep these decisions current. Finally, discuss what you might do to change these archaic decisions so that you are not held back by them.

     For example, you may have decided early on to keep all of your negative feelings inside of you, for you may have been told both directly and indirectly that you were unacceptable when you expressed negative feelings. In this case, you could discuss what you do now in situations where you experience negative feelings. Do you feel that you want to change your old decision?

5. Exploring your rackets. In TA, a "racket" refers to the collection of bad feelings that people use to justify their life script and the feelings on which they base their decisions. Some possible rackets are:

- an anger racket

- a guilt racket

• a hurt racket

• a depression racket

For instance, if you develop a depression racket you may actually seek out situations that will support your feelings of depression. You will continually do things to make yourself feel depressed, and thus you will feel this way enough of the time to be able to convince yourself that you are right to have these feelings.

In your group, spend some time exploring how you maintain old, chronic, bad feelings. What might be one of your major rackets? List some recent situations that you put yourself in or found yourself in that led to old, familiar feelings of depression, guilt, or the like.

6. Games we play. In this group exercise, devote some time to listing some of the games that you played as a child to get what you wanted. For example, perhaps you played the Helplessness Game. If you act helpless and pretend you cannot do something, then others may treat you as being helpless and do for you what you really don't want to do for yourself. Thus, if you did not want to make your own decisions as a child for fear of the consequences, you played stupid, and your parents then did for you what you were unwilling to do for yourself. True, you did get something from the game, but how does the price you paid compare with what you got?

In your group, discuss some games you played as a child, then list what you got from each game and the price you paid for the gains. What games do you play now? Discuss what you get from these games. Evaluate the costs. What do you think you'd be like if you gave up these games?

7. Life positions. Have each person in your group briefly describe him- or herself with respect to self-esteem. Do you genuinely like and appreciate yourself? Can you feel like a winner without putting another person down? Do you think you are right and the rest of the world is wrong? Or do you continually put yourself down?

Early in life you might have felt that everyone around you was just fine and that you were basically rotten to the core. What are some of the situations that led to these feelings of inadequacy? How might you challenge these feelings now? Would you classify yourself as a winner or a loser?

8. Changes in your life circumstances. You may have felt basically inadequate as a child, yet now you may feel very adequate in many areas of your life. What factors do you think are responsible for this shift in the way you feel about yourself?

9. A book of you. Write your own table of contents and list the chapters in the book about your life, and then give your book a title. What title best captures the sense of your life now? What would you include in the chapters? Mention the key turning points and key events of your life in your table of contents so that others in your group will have a picture of who you are. Now, assume you want to revise your book. What revisions do you want to make, chapter by chapter? Do you want a new book title?

10. "You are your parents" exercise. This exercise can be done with a partner or in small groups. It will provide a format for looking at the influence your parents have on you and the quality of life you see your parents experiencing, and it will help you to decide how you'd like to modify your own values and behavior.

   Close your eyes and see your parents at their present ages in a typical setting. Visualize the way they live. How is their marriage? How do they react to their children? What kind of life do they have? Now imagine yourself at their ages in the same setting. For a few minutes, imagine that you value what they do and that your life is almost identical with theirs. In what ways would you modify the outcomes of this fantasy?

11. Early decisions. Assume that you are a group leader and you identify that certain group members have made the following decisions. Speculate about what factors may have contributed to each of these decisions:

   • "I'll always be a failure."

   • "I'm basically weak and helpless."

   • "I won't feel, and that way I won't experience pain."

   • "Regardless of what I accomplish, I'll never be enough."

12. Redecision work in groups. Take the four statements above, and assume that each of them represents a life orientation. How would you proceed in working with each of these approaches toward life? What new decisions would you like to see be made? What would it take to change these decisions?

QUESTIONS FOR DISCUSSION AND EVALUATION

1. TA groups work on a contract basis, which means that members clearly specify what they want to change as well as what they are willing to do to change. What do you think of the use of contracts in groups? If you were to become involved as a client in a TA group, what are some contracts that you'd be willing to make? List one such contract, including a specific statement of some behavior you want to change and the steps you'd be willing to take to make this change.

2. In TA groups, emphasis is placed on working with injunctions, or parental messages that influence the way we behave. Can you see how some injunctions that you have internalized might have some effect on the manner in which you work with people in groups? Explain.

3. TA groups also work on expanding members' awareness of early decisions that they made about life, others, and themselves and challenge members to make new decisions. Do you really believe that most people are capable of redeciding? Why or why not? What forces may prevent people from going through what is necessary in order to make new decisions?

4. Discuss the possible combinations of TA with Gestalt. What concepts and techniques can be blended together? What value, if any, do you see from such a merger?

5. What is your personal evaluation of the TA approach to group work? Consider questions such as the following in your critique?

   • To what kind of clients do you think TA is best suited?

   • What contributions of TA do you think are most significant?

   • What are the major limitations of TA? Explain.

CHAPTER
12

Behavior Therapy

<u>Directions</u>: Refer to page 34 for general directions. Indicate your position
on these statements, using the following code:

   5 = I <u>strongly agree</u> with this statement.

   4 = I <u>agree</u>, in most respects, with this statement.

   3 = I am <u>undecided</u> in my opinion about this statement.

   2 = I <u>disagree</u>, in most respects, with this statement.

   1 = I <u>strongly disagree</u> with this statement.

_____ 1. Self-reinforcement is needed if participants hope to translate
          changes made in group to everyday life.

_____ 2. Assessment is a necessary step in the initial phase of a group.

_____ 3. Evaluation of results is best done continually during all the phases
          of a group.

_____ 4. For change to occur, members must actively participate in group
          work, and they must be willing to practice outside of group ses-
          sions.

_____ 5. Specificity in goal formation increases the chances that members
          will do productive group work.

STAGES IN THE DEVELOPMENT OF THE BEHAVIORAL THERAPY GROUP

Dimension	Initial Stage	Working Stage	Final Stage
Key developmental tasks and goals	The responsibilities and expectations of both the leaders and the members are outlined in a contract. Preparation of members is stressed. At the early stages the focus is on building cohesion, getting familiar with the structure of group therapy, and identifying problems to explore. Assessment is a vital aspect of the early sessions, as is setting of clear goals. A treatment plan, including procedures to be used to attain the stated goals, is developed and is constantly evaluated to test its effectiveness.	At this stage the treatment plan is implemented. A wide range of treatment procedures are used to solve specific problems and focus is on learning new skills. The central part of this phase is the work that is done outside of the group between sessions. The group is used as a place to learn and perfect new skills and to gain support and feedback so that progress continues. Much of the learning in the group takes place through modeling and observation, along with coaching. The emphasis is on behavior (changing unadaptive behavior or learning new skills) as opposed to the exploration of feelings.	At this phase the transfer of learning from the group to everyday life is critical. Situations that simulate the real world are used so that this transfer is facilitated. Focus is on learning ways of self-directed behavior and of developing plans for maintaining and using new coping skills. It is assumed that the generalization of learning will not occur by chance, so sessions are structured in such a manner that transfer of learning will be maximized.
Role of group leader and tasks	Leaders tasks are: to conduct pre-group interviews and screen members; organize the group; prepare the members by telling them how the group will work; establish group trust and cohesion; assess the nature of the problems to be explored; and provide a structure for the group. Leaders are active, and they provide information. They assist members in formulating specific goals.	Leaders develop an appropriate treatment plan based on the initial assessment, and they monitor those behaviors identified as problematic . They ongoingly assess progress and teach the members self-evaluation skills. Leaders reinforce desired behavior, and they assist members in learning methods of self-reinforcement. Leaders serve the function of modeling, coaching, and providing corrective feedback.	The main function of the leader at this phase is to assist members in learning ways to transfer new skills acquired in the group to situations in daily life. The leader prepares members for dealing with setbacks and teaches members skills needed to meet new situations effectively. The leader arranges for follow-up interviews to assess the impact of the group and to determine the degree to which members have fulfilled their contracts.
Role of group members	Members are involved in formulating the contract. They make a list of behaviors they want to change or they clarify the problems that they wish to work on in the group. They determine baseline data for certain behaviors and begin to monitor and to observe their behavior in the	The members report on the nature of their progress each week. Group time is used to define problem areas to work on in the group. Role playing of a behavioral nature is done to assist members in learning new skills. Members provide models for each other; they must carry out	The members decide what specific things they've learned in the group situation, and they practice new roles and behaviors, both in the group and in daily life. Feedback is provided so that skills and new behaviors can be refined, and suggestions are made for maintaining

	group as well. The members are involved in the assessment process, which continues throughout the group.	specific behavioral assignments, keep records of their progress, assess their progress in light of the baseline data collected at the initial sessions, and report to the group each week.	these new behavioral changes. The members act as a support system for each other. They typically agree to carry out specific assignments at the end of a group and then report back at a follow-up meeting.
Techniques	Basic techniques include contracts, checklists, role playing, and assessment devices.	Many behavioral techniques are used including reinforcement, modeling, densensitization, cognitive methods, and homework assignments.	Feedback is a main technique, as is role playing and developing self-reinforcement systems. Follow-up sessions are scheduled to assess outcomes.

Reactions: Summarize your reactions to the behavioral perspective on group developmental stages. What do you like most? Least? What aspects of this approach would you incorporate into your leadership style?

Questions: What questions about behavior therapy would you most like to raise and explore?

_____ 6. Part of the group leader's function is to provide reinforcement and to serve as a model.

_____ 7. Groups should aim at assisting participants to develop specific skills and self-directed methods of changing.

_____ 8. The group leader's attention to and interest in members serve as powerful sources of reinforcement.

_____ 9. Group members should decide on their own therapeutic goals.

_____ 10. Any group techniques or therapeutic procedures should be evaluated both by the group members and the leader to determine their effectiveness in meeting goals.

SUMMARY OF THE BASIC ASSUMPTIONS AND KEY CONCEPTS OF BEHAVIOR THERAPY IN GROUPS

1. Humans are shaped and determined by sociocultural conditioning. Behavior therapy is basically deterministic, in that it views behavior as the product of learning and conditioning.

2. Because all behavior is seen as the result of learning, the general therapeutic goal is to eliminate maladaptive behavior patterns by learning new, constructive patterns.

3. To accomplish this goal, the behavior therapist focuses on overt behavior, specifies treatment goals (which are usually decided by the client), and evaluates the results and outcomes.

4. The group therapist is active and directive, functioning in some ways as a trainer or teacher. All the techniques used by the group therapist are based on principles of learning and geared toward behavior change. Diagnosis, testing, and data gathering are frequently used techniques. The therapist is not interested in the client's past, unconscious material, or other internal states, rather he or she focuses on manipulating environmental variables.

5. The group members must actively participate in the group work and be willing to experiment with new behavior by taking a role in bringing about changes in behavior.

EXERCISES AND ACTIVITIES FOR THE BEHAVIORAL APPROACH TO GROUPS

Rationale

Behaviorally oriented group leaders have a variety of specific techniques that they can employ in group practice. These research-based techniques are systematically used to accomplish particular goals, and ongoing assessment is made by both the group members and the leader to determine whether or not the techniques being used are producing positive results. If members are not making progress, then the therapeutic procedures that are being used can be modified. It is basic to the behavioral approach that therapeutic procedures and evaluation of these techniques proceed simultaneously.

Most of the behavioral techniques are designed to effect specific behavioral changes—that is, either to decrease or eliminate undesirable behaviors or to acquire or increase desired behaviors. The following exercises will show you ways to apply learning principles in your work to change behavior. You can apply many of the techniques presented in these exercises to your own life. As you experiment with these techniques in your small groups or in class, determine which aspects of the behavioral approach you could incorporate into your work as a group leader, regardless of the theoretical model you might be working with.

Exercises

1. <u>Setting up a behavioral group</u>. Assume that you are a behaviorally oriented group leader and you are giving a talk to a community gathering where you hope to begin a group. What points would you emphasize to give these people a good picture of your group, your functions and role as a leader, and what would be expected of them as participants? Assume that they respond enthusiastically and want to join your group. Where would you begin, and how would you proceed in setting up this group? What pre-group concerns would you have? What would you do during the initial meeting?

2. <u>Terminating and evaluating a group</u>. Assume that the above group meets for 20 weeks. It is now the 18th week. What would you be concerned with as a group leader? Mention specific issues that you'd want the group to deal with. What kind of evaluation procedures would you employ at the end of the group? What kind of follow-up procedures would you use?

3. <u>Relaxation exercises</u>. Many behavioral group therapists use self-relaxation techniques; members are taught how to systematically relax every part of their bodies. They practice this in the group, and they also practice these relaxation exercises at home on a daily basis. In your own group, one of you can volunteer to lead a relaxation exercise using the tension-relaxation procedure, going from head to foot. After the exercise, discuss the possibilities for using relaxation procedures in any group. What are the values of such procedures? Consider practicing these relaxation exercises to reduce unnecessary stress. Give them at least a three-week trial to determine some personal benefits.

4. <u>Group desensitization methods</u>. Assume that you were asked to develop a group to work with college students who voluntarily want to deal with excessive anxiety that blocks their performance in test-taking situations. Show specifically what you'd do to create such a group, what procedures you'd use in the sessions, and how you'd evaluate the outcomes. Discuss such matters as teaching deep-relaxation methods, constructing a hierarchy, setting up imaginary scenes, and so on. Consult the textbook if you need to review specific procedures. For what <u>other</u> kind of problems do you think that systematic desensitization would be appropriate? Can you think of a certain problem that you have for which you could use this method? Discuss this in your group/class.

5. <u>Social reinforcement</u>. Observe in your own class or group how social reinforcement works. For example, for what are members reinforced? Pay attention to <u>nonverbal</u> responses, such as smiles, head nodding, and body
posture, as well as verbal support and approval. Do you see ways that you
can systematically use social reinforcmeent in a group situation? What
kind of social reinforcers have the most impact on your behavior? Support? Compliments? Applause?

6. <u>Modeling</u>. It is important for you to realize that, as a group leader, you
continually model behaviors for the members. What kind of behaviors would
you most want to model? Some that you might consider include clear and
direct speech, self-disclosure, respect, enthusiasm, sensitivity, and
caring confrontation. In your group, discuss ways that you can model
positive behavior. Also, observe the effect of a certain behavior on your
group (for example, speaking enthusiastically). Do you notice that members tend to assume some of the traits of the leader? What are the implications of this?

7. <u>Assertion-training groups: An introduction</u>. Assume that you are giving a
talk to people who might be interested in joining the assertion-training
group that you are forming. What would you tell them about your group?
What is <u>assertive behavior</u>? Whom is the group for? How can it help them?
What would they do in this group? What are some of the techniques that
you'd use during the group sessions? For this exercise, two of you in
your group can be the coleaders who are explaining all about the group
to the potential members; the others in the group can ask questions re-
lating to what they will be expected to do in the group, how this will
help them in daily life, and how they can apply what they learn.

8. <u>Applying assertive-training procedures to yourself</u>. In an exercise related to the preceding one, think of an area where you have difficulty
being assertive. This may involve dealing with supervisors, returning
faulty merchandise, or expressing positive feelings. In your own group,
you can experiment with improving your assertiveness in this area, using
specific procedures that are described in the textbook, such as behavior
rehearsal, role playing, coaching, cognitive restructuring, and so on.
Practice with these procedures <u>as a member</u> first, so that you can get
some idea of the values and applications of assertive-behavior training.

9. <u>Working on specific goals</u>. A real value of the behavioral approach is its
specificity—its ability to translate broad goals into specific ones.
State some broad/general goals that you'd like to attain. Then, in your
group, practice making these goals concrete. Make them specific to the
degree that you actually <u>know</u> what it is that you want and thus can
measure or evaluate progress toward them.
    As a second part of this exercise, assume that members in one of your
groups made global and vague statements such as the following. Can you
think of ways to make these goals clear and concrete?

a. "I'd like to be more spontaneous."

    Concrete goal is: _____

    _____

b. "I need to learn how to get in touch with my feelings."

Concrete goal is: _____

_____

c. "My goal is to become autonomous and an actualized person."

Concrete goal is: _____

_____

d. "There are a bunch of dumb fears I should get rid of."

Concrete goal is: _____

_____

e. "I'd like to be able to relate better."

Concrete goal is: _____

_____

f. "I'm all messed up, and I need a major overhaul."

Concrete goal is: _____

_____

g. "My goal is to get to know myself better."

Concrete goal is: _____

_____

10. <u>Groups designed for self-directed change</u>. Assume that you wanted to organize a group for people who were interested in self-directed change. For example, they may be interested in stopping smoking, taking weight off and keeping it off through a different diet and a physical exercise program, or changing their habits of self-discipline regarding study or work. How would you design a group of this nature?

11. <u>Applying a self-directed program to yourself</u>. In your group or class, discuss the specific behavior that you want to work on during the semester. Next, decide what you are willing to do to change this behavior. Draw up a specific contract and include details. (For instance, I will lose 10 pounds by the end of the semester, I will regulate eating habits, and I will ride a bicycle for an hour daily for the duration of the semester.) Then, during the remainder of the semester, practice your program and report your progress to your group. Ask a fellow student to support you if you get discouraged or find that you have difficulty sticking to your program.

You can apply self-directed behavioral modification methods to areas such as developing better patterns of organization, reducing stress through a program of meditation and relaxation exercises, changing what you consider to be negative behavior patterns, and so on.

12. Working with fears. Systematic desensitization is a useful technique for alleviating specific fears that you might have. Make a list of some of your fears. Are you afraid of certain animals? Are you afraid of failing in new situations? Are you afraid of heights? After you compile your list of fears, show how you might work with them in a group using the systematic desensitization procedure. How do you imagine this procedure would work for you?

13. Self-reinforcement methods. Behavioral-group work teaches members how to reinforce themselves so that they are not dependent on external rewards to maintain newly acquired skills. In your class/group, experiment with ways you can reinforce yourself after successes. Brainstorm this topic in your group.

   Self-reinforcement may involve learning ways to praise yourself and at the same time remind yourself of certain realities that you tend to forget. An example of this is writing notes to yourself and putting them on the mirror. These notes could say "You are worthwhile," "I am enough," "I have a right to my own feelings," "I'll like myself better if I treat myself with regard," "I can take time for myself." List some other examples of self-reinforcement methods:

_____

_____

_____

_____

_____

14. Personal evaluation and critique of behavioral groups. Discuss in your class/group what you consider to be the major strengths and weaknesses of the behavioral approach to groups. Consider such questions as:

   • What learning principles apply to all groups?

   • How can any group leader (regardless of theoretical orientation) draw on behavioral concepts and procedures?

   • How would you feel about using behavioral techniques as a group leader?

   • What are the limitations of behavior therapy?

   • What are your criticisms?

13

Rational-Emotive Therapy

PRECHAPTER PRIMER AND SELF-INVENTORY FOR
RATIONAL-EMOTIVE THERAPY IN GROUPS

<u>Directions</u>: Refer to page 34 for general directions. Indicate your position on these statements, using the following code:

5 = I <u>strongly agree</u> with this statement.

4 = I <u>agree</u>, in most respects, with this statement.

3 = I am <u>undecided</u> in my opinion about this statement.

2 = I <u>disagree</u>, in most respects, with this statement.

1 = I <u>strongly disagree</u> with this statement.

___5 1. It is primarily our beliefs that cause emotional disturbances; therefore, group work should focus on examining these beliefs.

___4 2. For group leaders to be effective, they need to be willing to challenge, confront, probe, and convince members to practice activities both inside and outside the group.

___5 3. It is the group leader's task to show members <u>how</u> they have caused and now perpetuate their emotional/behavioral problems.

___4 4. Group members have to be willing to discipline themselves by working hard both in and out of the group; they have to be active in confronting themselves.

STAGES IN THE DEVELOPMENT OF THE RATIONAL-EMOTIVE THERAPY GROUP

Dimension	Initial Stage	Working Stage	Final Stage
Key developmental tasks and goals	Key task is to teach members the A-B-C theory of how they create and uncreate their own disturbances, how to detect their irrational beliefs, and how to attack these faulty beliefs. Members need to learn that situations themselves do not cause emotional problems; rather, their beliefs about these situations cause the problems. Thus, changing beliefs (not situations) is the road to improvement.	Group focuses on the identification and attacking of members' musts, shoulds, and demands. Members learn that, if life is not the way they want it to be, this may be unfortunate but not catastrophic. In place of self-defeating assumptions, members incorporate beliefs that are grounded in reality.	Ultimate aim is that participants internalize a rational philosophy of life, just as they internalized a set of irrational beliefs. This phase is one of reinforcement of new learning to replace old patterns. Emphasis is on teaching people better methods of self-management.
Role of group leader and tasks	The group leader shows members how they have caused their own misery by teaching them the connection between their emotional/behavioral disturbances and their beliefs.	Leader acts as a counterpropagandist who confronts members with the propaganda they originally accepted without question and with which they continue to indoctrinate themselves. Leader strives to modify members' thinking by challenging their underlying basic assumptions about reality.	Therapist continues to act as teacher by showing members methods of self-control, giving them homework assignments that involve active practice in real life, and by correcting any lasting faulty patterns.
Role of group members	Members must be willing to discipline themselves and work hard, both during the sessions and between sessions. They must be active, both in and out of the group, for they learn by practicing and doing.	Members learn how to analyze, dispute, and debate by using scientific methods to question their belief systems. Members ask "What evidence supports my views?"	Group members integrate what they have learned and continue to make plans for how they can practice overcoming self-defeating thinking and emoting outside of the group.

Techniques	Educational methods: use of tapes, books, and lectures. Suggestions; information-giving; interpretation; group feedback and support. Other active-directive, confrontational, didactic, philosophic, and action-oriented methods.	A rapid-fire and forceful set of techniques, which emphasize cognitive factors, are used. These include use of persuasion, homework assignments, desensitization, role playing, modeling and imitation, behavior rehearsal, operant control of thinking and emoting, group feedback and support, cognitive restructuring, and assertive training.	Continued use of emotive-evocative and cognitive-behavioral techniques that people can use on their own after therapy terminates.

Reactions: Summarize your reactions to the rational-emotive approach to group developmental stages. What do you like most? Least? What aspects of this approach would you incorporate into your leadership style?

Questions: What questions about rational-emotive therapy would you most like to raise and explore?

97

_5_ 5. A leader serves the role of a counterpropagandist.

_5_ 6. A large part of the leader's task is to be a teacher, especially of how to detect and dispute irrational beliefs.

_4_ 7. Homework assignments are a valuable part of group counseling.

_5_ 8. Therapy is essentially a cognitive, active-directive, behavioral process.

_3_ 9. A major function of the group leader is to serve as a model.

_2_ 10. A warm and personal relationship between the group leader and the members is **not** essential to the group's success.

SUMMARY OF THE BASIC ASSUMPTIONS AND KEY CONCEPTS OF THE RATIONAL-EMOTIVE APPROACH TO GROUPS

1. People's belief systems cause emotional disturbances. Situations alone do not determine emotional disturbances, rather it is people's evaluations of these situations that are crucial.

2. People have a tendency to fall victim to irrational beliefs, and, although these beliefs were originally incorporated from external sources, people internalize and maintain these self-defeating beliefs by a process of self-indoctrination.

3. In order to overcome this indoctrination process that results in irrational thinking (which is the root of people's difficulties), group therapists use active-directive intervention methods, such as teaching, persuading, reindoctrinating, giving homework assignments, and so on, to get group members to challenge their beliefs and substitute a rational belief system for an irrational one.

4. The member/leader relationship is not stressed; rather, what is emphasized is the group therapist's skill in challenging, confronting, probing, and convincing the members to practice activities that will lead to positive change.

EXERCISES AND ACTIVITIES FOR THE RET APPROACH TO GROUPS

Rationale

The rationale underlying most of these exercises and RET techniques is that most of us make irrational assumptions about ourselves and the world that lead to emotional/behavioral disturbances. The essence of RET is that rational thinking can lead to more effective living. To combat stubborn and persistent irrational beliefs, it is necessary to work and practice diligently and to replace faulty thinking with logical thinking.

The following activities and exercises are designed to help you experience the process of challenging your own thinking and to become aware of the consequent feelings of your belief system. As you work through these exercises on your own, with another person, and with a small group, think about ways that, as a group leader, you could incorporate them into group practice.

Exercises

1. Make a list of a few self-defeating sentences that you tend to say to yourself. The purpose of this is for you to become aware of how <u>you</u> now continue to indoctrinate yourself with propaganda. Then take your self-defeating sentences and rewrite them in new and constructive ways, much like the example that follows:

    <u>Self-defeating sentence</u>. "I'm sure I'll be a failure as a counselor."
    <u>Constructive sentence</u>. "If I am willing to work diligently and apply myself to a good training program, then I'm sure that with experience I'll succeed."

    1a. Self-defeating sentence _____

    1b. Constructive sentence _____

    2a. Self-defeating sentence _____

    2b. Constructive sentence _____

2. Write <u>constructive sentences</u>, ones that you might suggest to a group member who repeated self-defeating sentences such as the following:

    1a. "I've always been stupid, and I suppose that I'll always be that way."

    1b. _____

    2a. "I need to please everyone, because rejection is just terrible."

    2b. _____

    3a. "Because my parents never really loved me, I guess nobody else could ever love me."

    3b. _____

    4a. "Basically, I'm simply an irresponsible person."

    4b. _____

3. <u>Self-rating</u>—giving yourself a "good" or "bad" evaluation based on your performances—can influence the way you think and feel. Ellis contends that the self-rating process constitutes one of the main sources of people's emotional disturbances. Discuss these questions in class or in a small group:

    a. What are some of the ways you rate yourself?

    b. How do you <u>feel</u> when you rate yourself critically?

4. <u>Homework assignments</u> are an integral part of RET group work. Think of your own patterns of behavior and ways that you'd like to think, feel, and behave more rationally. Then list a few specific homework assignments that you could do to challenge yourself to accomplish this. Carry out a few of these assignments and bring the results to your group. Ask for suggestions from your fellow students/group members. Below are a couple of examples of homework assignments that may be useful to you.

a. Do you have difficulties in making social contacts? Does it make you anxious to initiate a discussion with a member of the opposite sex? Do you want to feel more at ease in these situations than you do now? If so, try this experiment: go to each of your classes early and sit in a different place each time near a person that you don't know. Push yourself to initiate a conversation. Keep a record of all of the things, including irrational beliefs, you rehearse in your head before you make these contacts.

b. Are you troubled by conflicts with authority figures? For example, would you like to feel easier about approaching an instructor to discuss your progress in the course? If so, what stops you from selecting at least one instructor and making the time and effort to discuss with him or her matters that are of importance to you?

5. Think of some in-group practice assignments or homework exercises for members who demonstrate problems such as the following and write them down. Bring these assignments to class or group and share ideas with one another.

a. A woman says very little during the group sessions because she's afraid that she'll sound stupid and that other members would laugh at her. One possible assignment is:

_____

_____

_____

b. A woman believes that men are always judging her in a critical fashion. She avoids men both in the group and outside of group because she doesn't want to feel negatively judged. One possible assignment is:

_____

_____

_____

c. A young, unmarried man experiences a great deal of anxiety in asking women out on dates. Sometimes he'll avoid doing so, because he is afraid of being rejected or afraid of not knowing what to say to them if they were to accept. He'd like to overcome this avoidance behavior and lessen his anxiety. One possible assignment is:

_____

_____

_____

d. One of the members of a group you're leading tells you that he feels and believes that he _must_ gain universal approval. When someone is displeased with him, then he feels like a worm. Because of this he tries hard to figure out what every person in the group wants from him, and then he goes out of his way to meet these expectations. He says that he is sick of being the "super nice guy" and desperately wants to change. One possible assignment is:

_____

_____

_____

e. A member describes her drive to be perfect, and says that she carefully avoids situations and activities that make it difficult for her to feel that she's performed perfectly. She wants to relax and not be obsessed with the thought that she _must_ be perfect in anything she attempts. One possible assignment is:

_____

_____

_____

6. Role playing with a cognitive focus can be useful in an RET group. Think of a situation that causes you difficulty—one that you'd be willing to share in your group or class—and role play it. For example, you may feel victimized because you can't get your father's approval. Have a person play _your_ role as you first, and you role play your demanding father—the one who refuses to give approval no matter what is accomplished. After about five minutes or so, reverse roles: you be yourself while someone else plays your father as you portrayed him. Continue this for about another five minutes. Afterwards, do a _cognitive evaluation_ of this interchange in your group. Some questions you might include in your evaluation are:

• How did you appear to others as you played yourself in talking with your father?

• Do you _need_ his approval to survive?

• What will become of you if he never gives you his approval?

• What might you have to do to get his approval?

• How do you imagine you'd feel if you did what might be required to gain his acceptance?

- Can you gain self-acceptance, even if acceptance is not forthcoming from him?

- In what ways do you treat others like your father?

7. Imagine that you want to conduct an RET group in the agency or institution in which you work (or may someday work in the future). Convince your supervisor or the agency director of the advantages of doing RET in a group over doing it on an individual basis. What are some unqiue advantages of RET in groups, and why should your supervisor permit you to organize such a group? This can be a productive, as well as enjoyable, exercise that you can do in your group or class. Another student can play the role of the director/supervisor of the agency.

QUESTIONS FOR DISCUSSION AND EVALUATION

These questions can be used as a study guide as you read the corresponding chapter in the textbook, and they can provide discussion material for your class and small group.

1. Assume you are leading a group and you confront a member with what you think is clearly an irrational assumption and a self-defeating view on her part. The member responds with "Look, I know what I think is irrational. I know that all men aren't the bastard that my father was, and I keep telling myself this. Still, whenever I'm with a man I feel that he's out to take advantage of me and that he is just like my father." How might you proceed with this member who recognizes that her belief is faulty, yet can't seem to change her negative feelings?

2. Discuss how you think you'd function as an RET group counselor. RET is an active-directive, cognitive/behavioral, highly didactic method of therapy. Do you see any problems within yourself that might make it difficult for you to function in this manner? In your group or class, exchange ideas about specific aspects of RET that you'd find difficult to incorporate in your leadership style.

3. Do you think it is the group leader's place to teach the group members a philosophy of life? As a group leader, in challenging the belief systems of your clients, do you think that you can avoid imposing your values on them? Are there any values that you'd like to impose on the members of your groups? Do you think it is desirable to expose your values and beliefs to the group members? Do you think it is desirable to remain "value free" or "value neutral"? Discuss the reasons for your answers.

4. RET emphasizes cognitive processes. Do you think that enough attention is given to the emotional aspects of therapy? Do you think that self-defeating behavior can be eliminated exclusively by cognitive methods? Why or why not?

5. What dangers, if any, do you see for groups whose leaders function primarily within an RET perspective? Do you foresee any potentially harmful results that are more likely to occur with an RET approach than with less directive and active approaches?

CHAPTER
14

Reality Therapy

PRECHAPTER PRIMER AND SELF-INVENTORY FOR
REALITY THERAPY IN GROUPS

<u>Directions</u>: Refer to page 34 for general directions. Indicate your position
on these statements, using the following code:

5 = I <u>strongly agree</u> with this statement.

4 = I <u>agree</u>, in most respects, with this statement.

3 = I am <u>undecided</u> in my opinion about this statement.

2 = I <u>disagree</u>, in most respects, with this statement.

1 = I <u>strongly disagree</u> with this statement.

_____ 1. The group counselor's main task is to encourage the group members to
face reality and make value judgments regarding present behavior.

_____ 2. By emphasizing the unconscious, one avoids coming to grips with the
issue of one's irresponsibility.

_____ 3. Blaming others and making excuses for one's behavior leads to a
cementing of one's identification with failure.

_____ 4. Involvement is the core of therapy, for without it, there is no
therapy.

_____ 5. Group leaders should not focus on misery and failures; rather, they
should accentuate the members' strengths.

STAGES IN THE DEVELOPMENT OF THE REALITY THERAPY GROUP

Dimension	Initial Stage	Working Stage	Final Stage
Key developmental tasks and goals	First task is to create member-to-member relationships and a sense of involvement in the group; leader-to-member relationships based on trust are essential. Major goal of initial stage is to get members to look at the degree to which current behavior is meeting their needs.	Focus is on present behavior rather than feelings. Past is important only insofar as it influences present behavior. The central goal is to create a climate wherein members will learn to understand how their irresponsibility and poor choices have led to their current personal problems; in this way, members can establish "success" identities.	Specific plans for achieving desirable behavior patterns must be established; although plans are crucial for behavioral change to occur, a noncritical therapeutic milieu must be created in order to give members the strength to carry out their plans.
Role of group leader and tasks	Group leader has the task of fostering involvement among the members; he or she will encourage involvement by being active and involved with every member. Leader may question, ask others to make comments, and encourage interaction in the group. The modeling role is crucial. Leader focuses on current behavior and begins to get the members to look at what they get from their behavior.	Leader encourages members to evaluate their own behavior, asks members whether or not their current behavior is meeting their needs, and firmly rejects excuses and rationalizations. Counselor praises and approves responsible behavior. Counselor avoids labeling people with diagnostic categories.	Assists members in formulating realistic plans for change; creates a noncritical therapeutic climate that helps members to believe change is possible. Leader does not give up, even if members fail to carry out plans; he or she insists on finding a short-range plan that will lead to success.
Role of group members	Members focus on current behavior and problem areas. Focus may be on how each member attempts to gain love and feelings of self-worth and success. Members are expected to face their problems and to make plans to solve them.	Members evaluate own behavior and make value judgments about this behavior. Essential that members understand what they are doing as well as what they are getting from this behavior. Members must decide for themselves if they are willing to change their patterns of behavior.	Realistic plans must be made and carried out. Commitment is basic to following through with plans to change behavior.

Techniques	Building rapport, trust, and mutual respect; requesting information; involvement; task-orientation; conveyance of conditional acceptance and personal attitude.	Confrontation; insistance on importance of evaluating behavior and making decisions; avoidance of punishment.	Contracts; behavioral strategies, such as role playing, behavior rehearsal, homework assignments, and so on; encouragement and support.

Reactions: Summarize your reactions to the reality-therapy perspective on group developmental stages. What do you like most? Least? What aspects of this approach would you incorporate into your leadership style?

Questions: What questions about reality therapy would you most like to raise and explore?

_____ 6. The focus of group work should be on changing behavior, rather than on changing feelings or attitudes.

_____ 7. It is not the group leader's role to make value judgments for group members; rather, he or she should challenge them to evaluate their own behavior.

_____ 8. Insight is <u>not</u> essential to produce change.

_____ 9. Unless clients are willing to accept responsibility for their behavior, they will not be able to change their behavior.

_____ 10. The concept of responsibility implies meeting one's own needs in such a way that other people are not deprived of fulfilling their needs.

SUMMARY OF THE BASIC ASSUMPTIONS AND KEY CONCEPTS OF THE REALITY-THERAPY APPROACH TO GROUPS

1. We all have a need to develop a "success" identity, and one way of doing this is by living realistically and accepting responsibility for our behavior.

2. Mental health is equated with acceptance of responsibility, and the medical model of mental illness is rejected. Instead, value judgments and morality are stressed, and group members are challenged to evaluate the quality of their behavior. Focus is on present behavior, and the past is not emphasized.

3. Group leaders using reality therapy tend to focus on what group members can do now to change their behavior and on the means of doing so. These include being willing to make a commitment to change, developing a plan for action, and following through. Thus, group therapists do not explore the past, and they do not accept any excuses for the failure of members to follow through with their commitments.

4. Like behavior therapy, this approach is basically active, directive, and didactic, and it employs a contract method. The group therapist's main task is to encourage the members to face reality and make value judgments regarding present behavior. Thus, behavior is the focus, not attitudes, insight, or one's past or unconscious motivations.

EXERCISES AND ACTIVITIES FOR THE REALITY-THERAPY APPROACH TO GROUPS

Rationale

Some of the following exercises, activities, and questions can be used on your own, and others can be used in small groups. After you have worked with this material and answered the questions, you will be in a better position to know what and how much of these ideas you might want to employ in the groups you lead or will lead.

Exercises

1. Responsibility

   a. Responsibility is a major characteristic of reality therapy. What is
   your own view of responsibility? How, specifically, were you taught
   responsbility?

   b. Talk about how responsible you are right now in your life. What are
   some ways that you may attempt to dodge responsibility. How do you
   accept it?

   c. Do you blame others for the way you see yourself? In what ways do
   you attempt to put responsibility on external factors to justify the
   way you are? What would it be like for you to fully accept the responsibility for the way you are?

2. "Success" and "failure" identities

   a. What are some of your experiences that have contributed to the picture you have of yourself now? How did significant people react to
   you? What were their expectations of you? Mention at least three successes that you had as a child and as an adolescent. Mention three
   failures you experienced during these years. How do you think these
   successes and failures have influenced your current view of yourself
   as well as your feelings about your perspective?

   b. How does what you say about yourself affect the way people view and
   treat you? What self-fulfilling prophecies do you possibly subject
   yourself to? In what ways do you set yourself up for success or failure?

   c. If your parents were to describe you in terms of a success/failure
   identity, what might they say about you? What do you imagine your
   best friend would say? If you are in a group now, how do you think
   others perceive you?

   d. Is there a difference between the way you see yourself now and the
   way you'd like to be? If so, what changes would you like to make?
   In what ways do you restrict your possibilities by rigidly adhering
   to fixed notions that do not allow for change? Do you tell yourself
   that you can't be other than you are—that you can't change?

3. Value judgment and self-evaluation. What are some values that are important to you? What difficulties do you, as a group leader, predict that
   you'll have as a result of value clashes with group members? What kinds
   of clients do you think you could not effectively work with in a group
   because of a divergence in philosophy, life-style, and value system. Why
   would you have trouble working with them?

4. Involvement

   a. Do you think the group leader should become involved with the participants? Why or why not? How would you involve yourself in the groups

you will lead? With what kinds of clients would you most easily become involved? With what kinds of people would it be difficult for you to become involved?

b. Have your group divide into pairs. One person in each pair should play the role of a potential group member, and the other person should be the group leader and conduct a pre-session interview. How would you begin the process of getting involved? Demonstrate this with your partner. Give each other feedback, and take turns at being the "counselor" and the "client."

5. Developing a plan for change

a. What kinds of commitments would you, as a leader, expect from those who participate in your groups? What methods would you use to assist them in formulating specific action plans? How do you imagine that you'd handle participants who continually made plans but then returned to group without having followed through on most of them?

b. How would you, as a group member, deal with group members who talk about wanting to change but refuse to make any concrete plans to put into action outside the group. Perhaps they insist that they have never been able to make plans. What would you tell them?

QUESTIONS FOR DISCUSSION AND EVALUATION

1. The main task of the group leader, according to Glasser, is to encourage group members to face reality and to judge their own behavior and evaluate its consequences. In carrying out this task, counselors can't avoid getting involved with members in the realm of values and morality. This involvement raises a number of questions.

a. What is reality? Who defines reality—society? the counselor? the client? What if the client has a different view of reality than the counselor?

b. As a counselor, what are your criteria for judging what is acceptable and realistic behavior?

c. How might you, as a group counselor, work with a group of adolescents who refused to evaluate their behavior and who maintained that the only thing they wanted was to be released from the institution where they were sent by the Judge.

d. What problems might exist for you if the members of your group had a radically different background and different life-style from yours? Can you enter the world of reality of clients who have a life-style sharply divergent from your own?

2. Although Glasser maintains that counselors are not moralists (even though they recognize the exploration of morality as a vital part of the counseling process), he does believe that counselors should offer praise when clients act in responsible ways and show disapproval when they do not. He further maintains that clients demand this type of judgment; however, he

feels that counselors should teach clients that the key to finding happiness is to accept responsibility for making their own evaluations.

Glasser's position raises some central ethical questions, such as:

a. How fine is the line between merely challenging clients to assess their behavior and actively teaching them what they should value?

b. Do you think it's appropriate for a group counselor to talk openly about his or her values? Might this lead the members to incorporate the counselor's values, rather than develop their own values?

c. Or do you think it's better for counselors to keep their values "out of the counseling process?" Is this possible? Are there times when a group leader might want to impose certain values on the group instead of merely exposing these values? When? Why or why not?

3. What are the advantages and the limitations of reality therapy's strict emphasis on present behavior to the exclusion of exploring the client's past?

4. Do you agree with Glasser's concept that mental illness is the result of irresponsibility? Why or why not? Can you think of any other factors that are related to mental illness besides irresponsibility?

5. Reality therapy focuses on current behavior, not on insight, feelings, and attitudes. Do you agree that insight is not a prerequisite for change? Why or why not? Do you think that, if people change their behavior in constructive ways, they will automatically change their feelings? Is it necessary to change one's attitude before effectively changing one's behavior?

6. Glasser believes that the group leader should provide a model for group members to emulate. Do you agree with this? How could you decide whether or not the model you provide is worth emulating?

7. Glasser says that it's important for the group leader to focus on the group members' strengths and assets in counseling, as opposed to dwelling on their problems and shortcomings. What advantages and limitations do you see in this? How might focusing on group members' strengths and positive qualities help them to formulate realistic plans for change and be encouraged to following through with these plans?

8. According to Glasser, the notion of transference provides a way for therapists and group members to hide; it prevents real involvement from occurring between the client and the counselor. Do you agree or disagree with this view? If you agree with Glasser's view, how do you think this would affect your style of leading a group?

9. Like transference, the role of the unconscious is given little attention in reality therapy, in order to avoid giving clients excuses to avoid facing reality. Do you agree or disagree with this? What would be the advantages and disadvantages of emphasizing only conscious processes during group work?

10. Commitment is an essential part of reality therapy. As a group coun-
    selor, how might you assist people with "failure" identities who have
    trouble making and keeping the commitments necessary for change?

PART
III

Application, Integration,
and Basic Issues

Chapter 15
Illustration of a Group in Action:
Various Perspectives

Chapter 16
Comparisons, Contrasts, and Integration

Chapter 17
Professional and Ethical Issues
in Group Practice

Illustration of a Group in Action: Various Perspectives

GUIDELINES FOR CRITIQUING VARIOUS
APPROACHES TO GROUP THERAPY

The textbook's illustration of a group in action is designed to give you a general picture of how different group-counseling approaches could be applied to the same group. Thus, it gives you practical examples of the advantages and disadvantages of each approach. In your class or group, using the following questions as a guide, discuss what aspects you like best (and least) of each approach as it was presented in the textbook illustration. Then explore the ways to integrate several approaches in your own leadership style—to selectively borrow concepts and procedures from all of the therapies—and to begin developing your own theory of group counseling.

Psychoanalytic Orientation

Using this approach:

1. How could the group leader create a sense of trust in this group?

2. How would the members' resistance be explained? How would resistance be handled by the leader?

3. How would the leader work with any strong feelings that the members directed against him or her?

4. What would the group leader primarily focus on in this group?

Psychodrama

Using this approach:

1. How could the group leader "warm up" the group? (Would you use any of these techniques in your group work?)

2. What value would the group leader place on re-enacting past events or enacting anticipated situations? (What do psychodrama and the psychoanalytic approach have in common? How do they differ?)

3. How would the group leader work with relationship conflicts? (What can you draw from this and apply to your group work?)

Existential-Humanistic Therapy

Using this approach:

1. What would the group leader focus on in this group? (What would you focus on?)

2. How would the theme "I'm alive, but I feel dead" be explained and dealt with?

3. How would the group leader describe this group and explain the occurrences in it, as opposed to a group leader using the psychoanalytic approach?

4. How would the group leader deal with group members who found little meaning in life and who expressed suicidal thoughts? (How would you deal with these issues as a group leader?)

Person-Centered Therapy

Using this approach:

1. How would the leader attempt to create trust?

2. How would the group leader work with a member who expressed problems with loneliness?

3. How could the leader provide more direction? (Do you think this group or any particular members in it <u>need</u> more direction and structure than is illustrated?)

Gestalt Therapy

Using this approach:

1. How would the group leader work with the members of this group, as opposed to a person-centered group leader?

2. If a member in this group wanted to work on a dream that related to emptiness, how would the leader carry this out—as opposed to a psychoanalytic group leader? (Which method would you tend to use, and why?)

3. Would the group leader use many action-oriented therapeutic techniques? Why or why not?

4. Would the group leader focus mainly on experiencing moment-to-moment feelings? (How much emphasis do you think should be put on the cognitive aspects of group therapy?)

Transactional Analysis

Using this approach:

1. How would the leader work with a member's drinking problem—as opposed to a psychoanalytic leader?

2. Contracts will be made between the leader and the members. How do you think contracts will work in this group?

3. How could the group leader also draw on Gestalt-therapy techniques to obtain the maximum benefits for this group?

4. What role would examining old decisions and making new decisions play in this group's work?

Behavior Therapy

Using this approach:

1. How would the group leader begin the group? (What are the typical steps and sequences in the behavioral group?)

2. How would the leader work with this group—as opposed to a psychoanalytic leader? an existential leader? a Gestalt leader?

3. What kind of learning principles would the group leader employ in this group? (Discuss key learning principles such as reinforcement, modeling, feedback, and so on.)

4. How would the group leader work with a member who is very unassertive? (How would you work with such a problem?)

Rational-Emotive Therapy

Using this approach:

1. The techniques employed in group work will be directive and confrontational. Do you think such techniques could be effective in this group? Why or why not? (Would you be comfortable using these techniques in your own group?)

114

2. How could the group leader also draw on Gestalt-therapy techniques to obtain the maximum benefits for this group?

3. How would the leader deal with the member who fears rejection? (How would this differ from what the person-centered therapist would do?)

4. How would the leader deal with the member with a marriage problem? (How would this differ from what an RET therapist would do? what a leader using psychodrama would do?)

Reality Therapy

Using this approach:

1. How would the group leader respond to a member who blames his past for his current problems?

2. How would the leader get members to evaluate their current behavior? What if the members gave excuses? (What do you think of the role assumed by the reality therapist? Would it fit you? Why or why not?)

16

Comparisons, Contrasts, and Integration

QUESTIONS FOR DISCUSSION AND EVALUATION

A. Perspectives on Goals for Group Counseling

1. How does the theoretical orientation of a group practitioner influence the group's goals and the direction it takes?

2. In view of the many differences among the various theoretical approaches to group therapy, how is it possible for there to be a common ground among behavioral-oriented groups and experiential- and relationship-oriented groups? How can long-range goals and concrete short-term goals be integrated into group practice?

3. As a group leader, what value would you place on the freedom of members to select personal goals? How would you bring the members' goals and the goals you have for the group into agreement? What problems can you foresee if these goals do not agree?

4. How do a group's goals relate to its type of membership?

5. Consult the comparative overview chart of group-therapy goals in the text. After you review these goals, complete the following outline:

   In your own words, state what you consider to be the central goal of each of these models:

   a. Psychoanalytic: _____

   _____

b. Psychodrama: _____

_____

c. Existential-Humanistic: _____

_____

d. Person-Centered: _____

_____

e. Gestalt: _____

_____

f. TA: _____

_____

g. Behavior Therapy: _____

_____

h. RET: _____

_____

i. Reality Therapy: _____

_____

Which model comes closest to your thinking? Which model do you disagree with most strongly? As you review the models, determine which goals you'd choose to incorporate into your own group-counseling theory.

B. The Role and Functions of the Group Leader

1. In the text, review the summary/overview chart that compares the various theoretical approaches to the role and function of the group leader. Then give a one-sentence description of what you think is the central role/function of the group leader from the point of view of each of these models?

a. Psychoanalytic: _____

_____

b. Psychodrama: _____

_____

c. Existential-Humanistic: _____

_____

d. Person-Centered: _____

_____

e. Gestalt: _____

_____

f. TA: _____

_____

g. Behavior Therapy: _____

_____

h. RET: _____

_____

i. Reality Therapy: _____

_____

2. After reviewing your summary above, write down the specific roles and functions that you think you will use as a group leader.

_____

_____

_____

_____

3. If you were asked in a job interview to describe in one sentence what you considered your central role to be as a group leader, what would you say?

_____

_____

_____

4. As a group leader, you have many functions. Rank order (from 1 being "most important" to 10 being "least important") the following ten group-leader roles:

_____ Facilitator

_____ Therapist

_____ Teacher

_____ Challenger

_____ Evaluator

_____ Technical expert

_____ Participant-observer

_____ Director

_____ Catalyst

_____ Program manager/organizer

5. Review the different stages in the development of a group. How do the group leader's roles change during these stages?

C. The Issue of Structuring and the Division of Responsibility

1. It is clear that a group leader will provide structure for the group. What is not predetermined is the degree and kind of structure he or she provides. The group could range from being extremely unstructured (the person-centered group) to being highly structured and directive (behavioral group). Review the chart in the textbook on degree of structuring and division of responsibility. Which theories come closest to your view? Why? What theories do you disagree with? Why? How could you combine some of these different approaches to structuring a group? How can these models stimulate your thinking regarding what type and degree of structuring you want to provide a group? How does structuring relate to the group's stage of development?

2. The division of responsibility, like structuring, can differ widely, according to the theoretical approach used in a group. Some therapies stress the group leader's responsibility in that they place primary responsibility on him or her for the direction and outcome of the group. Other therapies give primary responsibility to the group members and tend to downplay the role of the group leader. What is your position on this matter?

3. The group leader must always maintain a balance between taking on too much responsibility for the group and denying that he or she has any responsibility for its direction. What problems do you foresee for a group if the leader assumes either too much or not enough responsibility?

4. Review the chart in the textbook on the division of responsibility, and then give a one-sentence summary of the position taken by each of these models:

a. Psychoanalytic: _____

_____

b. Psychodrama: _____

_____

c. Existential-Humanistic: _____

_____

d. Person-Centered: _____

_____

e. Gestalt: _____

_____

f. TA: _____

_____

g. Behavior Therapy: _____

_____

h. RET: _____

_____

i. Reality Therapy: _____

_____

5. What do each of the above therapeutic approaches to responsibility offer to you as a group practitioner? Would you, as a group leader, want to assume more responsibility at some stages of a group than at others?

D. The Group Leader's Use of Technique

1. Review the overview chart in the textbook on group-therapy techniques. Then write down the specific technique(s) from each group theory that you find most useful.

a. Psychoanalytic: _____

_____

b. Psychodrama: _____

_____

c. Existential-Humanistic: _____

_____

d. Person-Centered: _____

_____

e. Gestalt: _____

_____

f. TA: _____

_____

g. Behavior Therapy: _____

_____

h. RET: _____

_____

i. Reality Therapy: _____

_____

2. Which techniques would you select and combine to use when you lead a group? How may each of these techniques be adapted to lead different kinds of groups? Write down the techniques that you think best fit the kind of person you are:

_____

_____

_____

_____

_____

_____

_____

_____

3. In order to learn more about how you use techniques, answer the following questions with "yes" or "no" (give your immediate response).

_____ a. Do you use techniques as catalysts?

_____ b. Are you eager to acquire many specific techniques to deal with specific problems that might arise in the group?

_____ c. Do you see techniques as gimmicks?

_____ d. Can you give reasons for using the techniques you choose?

_____ e. Do you think techniques should be used to get group members moving when they appear to be at an impasse?

_____ f. Do you borrow techniques from many approaches?

_____ g. Do you believe that the use of techniques can interfere with group process?

_____ h. Would you employ techniques designed to tap unconscious processes?

_____ i. Are you in favor of using structured and preplanned techniques to get the group to do something?

_____ j. Would you want to use action-oriented techniques?

_____ k. Do you do a lot of interpreting—telling group members the possible meaning of their behaviors?

_____ l. Would you want to teach members self-control and self-management techniques (such as stress reduction) that they could use outside of group?

_____ m. Would you want to use techniques that are highly directive, confrontational, and challenging?

_____ n. Do you agree that techniques are no less significant to group process than the group leader's personality and the relationship he or she has with group members?

_____ o. Do you rely on the use of techniques to give direction to a session?

_____ p. Do you think that it's necessary for a group leader to experience a technique him- or herself before using it in the group?

_____ q. Do you think that group leaders can keep themselves "hidden" as persons through the use of techniques?

_____ r. Would you tend to use techniques because you are anxious about not knowing what to do as a leader?

_____ s. Should clients be informed about the purpose of a technique?

_____ t. Do you think members should know, in advance of joining a group, about the types of techniques that are likely to be employed?

_____ u. Would you be inclined to use nonverbal techniques?

_____ v. Would you be inclined to use structured communication exercises in the group as a catalyst for interaction?

_____ w. Should a technique be an extension of who you are as a person—that is, a personal expression and not a mechanical exercise?

_____ x. Do you encourage members to suggest techniques for group interaction?

_____ y. Is it essential that techniques be geared to the nature and purpose of a specific group?

_____ z. Do you agree that you can reduce the chances of falling into a mechanical group-leadership style by deliberately paying attention to the _way_ you use techniques?

4. Look over the inventory above and circle the letters of the questions that you'd most like to explore in class.

Professional and Ethical Issues in Group Practice

A REVIEW OF BASIC ISSUES: A SELF-INVENTORY

The following multiple choice self-inventory is presented as a device for clarifying your values, beliefs, and attitudes insofar as they affect your leadership style. There are no "right answers"; this inventory is designed to stimulate thought and help you formulate your own positions on many of the ethical and professional issues that you are likely to encounter as a group practitioner.

After you complete this inventory I suggest that you note the items that produced the strongest responses in you and bring them up in class/group. Use this inventory any way you can to stimulate debate and open discussion in your class/group.

Circle the letter beside the response that most closely reflects your viewpoint at this time. Circle as many responses as you wish; if you don't like any of the responses provided, then write your own response on the blank line.

1. Is it possible for the group leader to keep his or her values out of the counseling situation and remain neutral?

    a. Yes, I think this is desirable.

    b. No, I don't think this is either desirable or possible.

    c. I think this would negatively affect the counseling relationship.

    d. I think this would be basically dishonest.

    e. _____

2. Which of the following comes closest to your viewpoint?

   a. It is the counselor's function to teach values.

   b. It is the counselor's function to expose his/her values.

   c. Counselors should challenge clients to question their values.

   d. Counselors should keep their values hidden so as not to unduly influence the client.

   e. _____

3. To what degree do you have a need for your clients to adopt your values?

   a. I'd like it if they did.

   b. I will counsel in such a manner as to encourage my clients to accept and embrace my values as their own.

   c. I would take steps to see that they would not merely accept my values as their own without thinking them through.

   d. _____

4. What role do you see values playing in the therapeutic process?

   a. Values are the core of the counceling process.

   b. Values basically direct the course of therapy, for they determine the goals and procedures of counseling.

   c. Both the client and the counselor should discuss values that influence therapy.

   d. Values can be effectively kept out of the client/therapist relationship.

   e. _____

5. What do you think of the position that counseling ought to deal with the issues of morality, right and wrong conduct, and value judgments?

   a. I strongly agree with the position.

   b. I somewhat agree.

   c. I somewhat disagree.

   d. I strongly disagree.

   e. _____

6. In which of the following ways do you think you are most likely to influence your clients?

   a. I might encourage them to talk about areas that I deem important.

   b. I'd give them a lot of reinforcement when they did things or said things I approved of.

   c. I'd pay closer attention to them when they were exploring topics that I thought were relevant.

   d. I'd work at not influencing them.

   e. _____

7. What is your opinion of the view that the role of the therapist should be to attack the value systems of clients that are irrational and to depropagandize these clients with rational thoughts?

   a. I strongly agree with this position.

   b. I somewhat agree.

   c. I somewhat disagree.

   d. I strongly disagree.

   e. _____

8. If a middle-aged man who complained of meaninglessness in life was seriously thinking about suicide because, no matter where or how he searched, he still felt empty, what would you do?

   a. I'd do everything possible to convince him not to kill himself.

   b. If I thought he were serious, I'd arrange to have him hospitalized in order to prevent this.

   c. I'd support his choice if it appeared that is what he really wanted.

   d. I'd do my best to refer him to another counselor.

   e. _____

9. What value do you place on security?

   a. Security should be a major factor in decision making.

   b. Generally, I'd encourage people to take risks even at the expense of losing security if growth seemed possible.

   c. Generally, I'd encourage people to keep what they have, if it isn't making them miserable.

   d. I am convinced that seeking security leads to complacency.

   e. _____

10. What criteria do you use to determine your sexual values and sexual ethics?

    a. I base my values on the teachings of a church or on the Bible.

    b. I attempt to be honest with myself by doing what I think is right.

    c. Whatever consenting adults agree on in the area of sexual behavior seems right to me.

    d. People should do whatever they feel like doing.

    e. _____

11. Which statement comes the closest to identifying your values concerning religion?

    a. Religion is a major force in my life.

    b. I consider myself religious, even though I don't belong to any organized religion.

    c. I think religion is a security blanket and, as such, it is made of myths.

    d. I think that religion encourages people to look outside of themselves for answers.

    e. _____

12. If you were aware of a major value conflict between your client and you, what do you think you would do?

    a. I'd refer the person to someone else.

    b. I'd work with the person and try to resolve the conflict.

    c. I'd seek consultation from a colleague or a supervisor.

    d. I'd tell the client my position and then let him or her decide whether or not he or she wanted to work with me.

    e. _____

13. What is your position on abortion?

    a. I believe in the right to life and I consider abortion to be morally wrong.

    b. I think it is a better alternative to bringing an unwanted child into the world.

    c. I believe that this is strictly up to the pregnant woman to make this decision.

    d. I think abortion should be legal and financed by the government for those who feel they need it.

    e. _____

14. What is your view of homosexuality?

    a. I see it as an expression of an emotional problem.

    b. I see it as being an acceptable way of life for those who choose it.

    c. I think people ought to experience it before they criticize this sexual proclivity.

    d. I think that people are naturally heterosexual and that homosexuality is generally the result of bad experiences with heterosexuality.

    e. _____

15. What has been the chief source of your present value system?

    a. I've acquired most of my values from my parents.

    b. Most of my values have resulted from introspection.

    c. I have largely accepted the values of the society in which I live, including those of my friends and colleagues.

    d. Religion has been the main source of my values.

    e. _____

16. How would you determine if clients are benefiting from group counseling?

    a. I'd ask them if they thought they were progressing.

    b. I'd use various types of personality tests.

    c. I'd look for evidence of actual changes in their behavior outside the session.

    d. I'd rely on my intuition or my judgment.

    e. _____

17. What would you use to determine whether or not you were competent to work with certain kinds of clients?

    a. I'd use my own judgment.

    b. If I had a degree or license, then I would be competent.

    c. I'd let my supervisor decide.

    d. I'd let the client decide.

    e. _____

18. What do you think about the issue of continuing education for licensed professionals:

    a. Once persons are licensed, they shouldn't have to take any more courses or workshops.

    b. I think it should be a requirement to have some kind of ongoing education as a condition for license renewal.

    c. Agencies ought to provide in-service programs for all the professionals who work there.

    d. I think it should be recommended, but not required.

    e. _____

19. What is unethical behavior on the part of a therapist?

    a. Any actions that are contrary to the established ethical codes of a professional organization.

    b. Anything that harms a client or is not in the best interest of the client.

    c. Behavior that the therapist judges to be unethical.

d. When therapists meet their needs at the expense of the client.

e. _____

20. Under what conditions would you violate confidentiality?

a. Only when I would be obliged to legally.

b. If I believed my client would harm another or himself/herself.

c. If I were frightened for my own safety.

d. If I found out that the client was engaging in unlawful actions.

e. _____

21. What criteria would you use to decide when to violate confidentiality?

a. Consultation with my colleagues.

b. Trusting my own intuitions.

c. Seeking direction from a supervisor.

d. Following the policy of the agency I work for.

e. _____

22. What is your view of sexual intimacy between a client and a therapist?

a. It is always unethical.

b. Under some circumstances, it could be beneficial for clients.

c. It is an exploitation of the client, and it hurts the client.

d. It is impossible to effectively combine a sexual relationship with a therapeutic one.

e. _____

23. What is your position on the issue of therapists having social relationships with clients?

a. It is unethical and unprofessional.

b. It strictly depends on the therapist to make the judgment whether or not it would interfere with therapy.

c. It could be very useful to build trust and a good social relationship.

d. It depends on the client.

e. _____

24. What is your view of nonerotic physical contact with clients?

a. It is dangerous and can easily lead to overt sexual behavior.

b. It can be very useful therapeutically.

c. There are more disadvantages than advantages to it.

d. It is therapeutically useful only when it is done authentically by a therapist.

e. _____

25. How do you think you would deal with a client to whom you became extremely sexually attracted?

   a. I might act on these feelings if I thought it wouldn't harm the client.

   b. I'd refer the client to another therapist and tell the client the reason for the referral.

   c. I'd accept my feelings as natural, but I probably would seek consultation.

   d. I'd honestly discuss with my client what I felt.

   e. _____

26. Which of the following do you think is the most serious form of unethical behavior?

   a. Needlessly breaking confidentiality.

   b. Consciously keeping a client dependent for personal reasons.

   c. Having sexual relations with a client.

   d. Working with clients with whom one is clearly not competent to deal.

   e. _____

27. What criteria would you use to develop your own professional code of ethics?

   a. I'd rely on the established codes and standards.

   b. I'd do whatever felt right and appropriate to me.

   c. I'd discuss questions and issues with colleagues I trusted.

   d. I would discuss any questionable behaviors with clients.

   e. _____

28. If you were to lead a group that included children or adolescents, would you secure the written permission of their parents?

   a. Yes, because it is legally sound to do so.

   b. Yes, because ethically this is essential.

   c. Yes, because it is a practical and politically wise idea.

   d. No, because it is really not necessary.

   e. _____

29. What is your view of members' socializing outside of group?

    a. I am opposed to it, for I think a group is for therapy, not for making friends.

    b. I think it can help make a group more real and can provide good material for discussion in group.

    c. It depends on the effect it has on the group.

    d. It depends on the level of maturity of the group members.

    e. _____

30. What is your view of group pressure (when several members in a group apply pressure to one individual in the group)?

    a. It's unethical.

    b. It's a most useful and appropriate measure to break down defenses.

    c. Group pressure is inevitable; it depends on how it is dealt with and the effect it has on members.

    d. _____

31. What is your view of screening members for a group.

    a. Ethical practice demands it.

    b. Generally, it is a waste of time.

    c. In screening, it is important that the group leader rely on his or her intuitive feeling about including or excluding a person from the group.

    d. It's good to present information about what the group is about, answer questions, and then allow the prospective participant to make the decision to join or not.

    e. _____

32. Which of the following do you consider to be the greatest psychological risk in group participation?

    a. Being pressured and forced to "open up."

    b. Being left hanging at the end of a group experience.

    c. Opening up feelings that are not worked through properly.

    d. Looking to other members to make one's own decisions.

    e. _____

33. What steps would you take to protect a group's confidentiality?

    a. I'd get members to sign a contract agreeing not to talk outside of group about what goes on in the group.

    b. I would tape-record all sessions.

    c. I would often bring this up as a topic for discussion.

d. I would do very little, and instead let the group itself deal with this issue in the way they see fit.

e. _____

34. What professional responsibility do you think group leaders have to demonstrate the effectiveness of their groups?

a. They should conduct research to determine if the group is effective or not.

b. Ethical practice demands some attempt to study the outcomes.

c. It is very difficult, if not impossible, to adequately demonstrate whether or not a group is effective.

d. _____

35. On the issue of training of group leaders, what statement comes closest to your view?

a. Group leaders should receive training that is determined by the profession they belong to.

b. Anyone with sensitivity and caring can be a good group leader, and formal training is not necessary.

c. Training should be ongoing and never end.

d. _____

36. How professional or ethical do you think it is for a group leader to occasionally use group time to discuss and explore his or her own personal problems in the group?

a. This is almost always unwise and it is unprofessional.

b. Anytime leaders take the focus off members, they are behaving unethically.

c. This kind of behavior means that the person is not ready to lead groups.

d. This can be a very useful way to model, and it can actually make the leader more effective.

e. _____

37. Should the group leader expect group members to take an active part in all of the group exercises?

a. Group members should always be free to decline to participate in any activity they choose to.

b. If members agree to join a group, they should not be allowed to "cop out" by not participating in a group activity.

c. If members decide not to participate in an exercise, they should state their reasons for not wanting to participate.

d. _____

38. Which form of community education do you think is the most important function of a professional counselor?

   a. The demystification of psychotherapy.

   b. Correcting erroneous notions about mental and emotional illness.

   c. Giving people information about how to use psychological services.

   d. Simply letting people know what help is available.

   e. _____

39. What do you think is the best way to educate a community about the nature of mental health and the available psychological services?

   a. Writing articles in the local newspaper.

   b. Finding out the sources of power in a community and contacting them.

   c. Making direct contact with people by talking at organizational meetings.

   d. _____

40. Which of the following factors do you think would be most likely to lead to burn out for you?

   a. Failing to have meaningful relationships in life.

   b. Assuming an inordinate degree of responsibility for counseling outcomes.

   c. Getting involved in political hassles in work.

   d. Working with clients who are unmotivated.

   e. _____

41. What do you see as the one best way to prevent burn out?

   a. Doing things that are enjoyable besides working.

   b. Finding ways to bring variety to work.

   c. Giving first priority to my personal life and finding satisfaction in intimate relationships.

   d. Refusing to take on too many work assignments.

   e. _____

42. As a counselor, if you experienced countertransference feelings toward a client, how might you interpret this?

   a. As a sign that I need further therapy.

   b. As a very normal and typical reaction of most counselors.

   c. As something that should be worked on with a colleague or a consultant.

   d. As a sign that this client evoked feelings in me similar to those evoked by significant people in my past.

   e. _____

43. Which of the following do you think is most important in a counselor's professional development?

   a. Practical field experience with supervision.

   b. Formal course work in theory and practice of counseling.

   c. Practice conducting experiential groups and other forms of personal therapy.

   d. _____

44. Which of the following do you consider to be the most important in the professional development of a counselor?

   a. Development of specific counseling and relationship skills.

   b. Awareness and sensitivity of ethical/professional issues.

   c. Cognitive knowledge of personality development and counseling theory.

   d. The counselor's personal development.

   e. _____

45. Which of the following measures best determines a group leader's level of competence?

   a. Possession of a license or credential as a mental-health practitioner.

   b. Completion of a broad background of course work in the theory and practice of counseling.

   c. Supervised practice.

   d. Affiliation with a professional organization.

   e. _____

46. What is your position on requiring candidates who expect to become group leaders to obtain experience as group members during their training?

   a. It should be left strictly up to the individual to decide if he or she needs or wants personal group experience.

   b. It should be a stipulation for licensure or attaining an advanced degree in counseling.

   c. If the candidate has serious problems, then it should be either recommended or required.

   d. It should be strongly recommended for all group-counselor trainees.

   e. _____

47. What is your view of requiring group-counselor candidates to participate in leaderless and self-directed groups as part of their training?

   a. This should be a part of a counselor training program.

   b. This should be required, because people only learn how to lead by practicing with peers.

c. Groups such as these, without a professional leader, should be discouraged.

d. This can be used profitably as an adjunct to participation in regular groups with professional leaders to develop autonomy and leadership skills.

e. _____

48. What is your position on using structured exercises in groups?

a. They are best avoided, because they tend to foster member dependency on the leader.

b. They can be very useful as catalysts to get people interacting with one another.

c. Group leaders should always have good reasons for using structured exercises and be able to explain the purpose of these technqiues to the group members.

d. They should be used when the group begins to lose vitality.

e. _____

49. What is your position concerning nudity as a part of certain types of groups?

a. It should be generally avoided, because it borders on unethical practice.

b. Nudity can be a valuable part of some groups; however, members should be given warning in advance.

c. Each group should take a vote and let the majority rule.

d. It is almost always counterproductive and should not be a part of any group.

e. _____

50. What comes closest to your view on the professional responsibility of a leader to provide some type of follow-up activity for a group, once the group ends?

a. It is clearly unethical to fail to offer a follow-up session after a group's termination.

b. This matter should be left for the group members to decide.

c. It might be a poor practice, for it could foster a dependent attitude on the members' part.

d. It could easily be a way for the group leader to avoid dealing with his or her feelings of separation and termination of the group.

e. _____

ETHICAL GUIDELINES FOR GROUP LEADERS
AND GUIDELINES FOR TRAINING GROUP LEADERS

The following documents on <u>Ethical Guidelines for Group Leaders</u> and <u>Guidelines for Training Group Leaders</u> were developed by the Association for Specialists in Group Work (ASGW) for use by its members, under the consecutive Presidencies of Merle Ohlsen, John Vriend, Allan Dye, and Walter Lifton. This working draft will undergo further revisions before it becomes officially adopted as association policy.

Interested persons who wish to join ASGW, a division of the American Personnel and Guidance Association, or who wish to obtain copies of these documents may write to:

> Jeffrey A. Kottler, Chairperson
> Professional Ethics and Standards Committee
> Association for Specialists in Group Work
> A.P.G.A. Headquarters
> Two Skyline Place
> 5203 Leesburg Pike
> Falls Church, Va. 22041

In my classes, I have students form small groups to discuss and evaluate the guidelines. After the students have had the time to go over most of the guidelines, each group presents its conclusions to the entire class. We focus on the issues that seem to generate the greatest degree of controversy. My students have argued with some of the points, thought that certain guidelines were incomplete, and found that modifications (expansions or deletions) were needed in some cases.

At the time when the ethical guidelines were being developed, the ASGW asked for feedback from interested persons. I pooled my class's comments, and we sent specific recommendations for revision to the Chairperson (Dr. Jeffrey Kottler). Some of these suggestions were apparently incorporated into the documents that follow. Your class might want to do the same thing. Guidelines such as these should be continually evaluated and refined. The guidelines are comprehensive and represent many months of collective thought and discussion, and I think they provide some direction for group workers in developing a sense of professionalism.

Study the following guidelines and circle the items that interest you most. Bring these items to class for discussion and debate. What ethical guidelines do you think are most important? What ethical guidelines, if any, do you disagree with? Do you think there are some guidelines that should be added to this document? What are your reactions to the guidelines for training standards for group leaders? How do these standards of training in clinical group practice compare with your own views of training and your own experience in being trained as a group leader? You might consider sending the results of your class discussions of these documents to the Chairperson of the ASGW.

ETHICAL GUIDELINES FOR GROUP LEADERS
Association for Specialists in Group Work

Preamble

One characteristic of any professional group is the possession of a body of knowledge and skills and mutually acceptable ethical standards for putting them into practice. Ethical standards consist of those principles which have been formally and publically acknowledged by the membership of a profession to serve as guidelines governing professional conduct, discharge of duties, and resolution of moral dilemmas. In this document, the Association for Specialists in Group Work has identified the standards of conduct necessary to maintain and regulate the high standards of integrity and leadership among its members.

The Association for Specialists in Group Work recognizes the basic commitment of its members to the Ethical Standards of its parent organization, the American Personnel & Guidance Association, and nothing in this document shall be construed to supplant that code. These standards are intended to complement the APGA standards in the area of group work by clarifying the nature of ethical responsibility of the counselor in the group setting and by stimulating a greater concern for competent group leadership.

The following ethical guidelines have been organized under three categories: the leader's responsibility for providing information about group work to clients, the group leader's responsibility for providing group counseling services to clients, and the group leader's responsibility for safegarding the standards of ethical practice.

A. **Responsibility for Providing Information About Group Work and Group Services:**

A-1. Group leaders shall fully inform group members, in advance and preferably in writing, of the goals in the group, qualifications of the leader, and procedures to be employed.

A-2. The group leader shall conduct a pre-group interview with each prospective member for purposes of screening, orientation, and, insofar as possible, shall select group members whose needs and goals are compatible with the established goals of the group; who will not impede the group process; and whose well-being will not be jeopardized by the group experience.

A-3. Group leaders shall protect members by defining clearly what confidentiality means, why it is important, and the difficulties involved in enforcement.

A-4. Group leaders shall explain, as realistically as possible, exactly what services can and cannot be provided within the particular group structure offered.

137

A-5. Group leaders shall provide prospective clients with specific information about any specialized or experimental activities in which they may be expected to participate.

A-6. Group leaders shall stress the personal risks involved in any group, especially regarding potential life-changes, and help group members explore their readiness to face these risks.

A-7. Group leaders shall inform members that participation is voluntary and that they may exit from the group at any time.

A-8. Group leaders shall inform members about recording of sessions and how tapes will be used.

B. <u>Responsibility for Providing Group Services to Clients:</u>

B-1. Group leaders shall protect member rights against physical threats, intimidation, coercion, and undue peer pressure.

B-2. Group leaders shall refrain from imposing their own agendas, needs, and values on group members.

B-3. Group leaders shall insure that each member has the opportunity to utilize group resources and interact within the group by minimizing barriers such as rambling and monopolizing time.

B-4. Group leaders shall treat each member individually and equally.

B-5. Group leaders shall abstain from inappropriate personal relationships with members throughout the duration of the group and any subsequent professional involvement.

B-6. Group leaders shall help promote independence of members from the group in the most efficient period of time.

B-7. Group leaders shall not attempt any technique unless thoroughly trained in its use or under supervision by an expert familiar with the intervention.

B-8. Group leaders shall not condone the use of alcohol or drugs directly prior to or during group sessions.

B-9. Group leaders shall make every effort to assist clients in developing their personal goals.

B-10. Group leaders shall provide between-session consultation to group members and follow-up after termination of the group, as needed or requested.

C. **Responsibility for Safeguarding Ethical Practice:**

C-1. Group leaders shall display these standards or make them available to group members.

C-2. Group leaders have the right to expect ethical behavior from colleagues and are obligated to rectify or disclose incompetent, unethical behavior demonstrated by a colleague by taking the following actions:

a. To confront the individual with the apparent violation of ethical guidelines for the purposes of protecting the safety of any clients and to help the group leader correct any inappropriate behaviors.

b. If the colleague refuses to alter his/her unethical behavior and/or rectify any accrued negative results, a formal complaint should be filed with the Chairperson of the ASGW Ethical and Professional Standards Committee. Such a complaint should be made in writing including the specific facts of the alleged violation and all relevant supporting data. A copy of the complaint shall be furnished to the charged member.

c. If it is determined by the Ethics and Professional Standards Committee that the alleged breach of ethical conduct constitutes a violation of the "Ethical Guidelines," then an investigation will be started by at least one member of the Committee plus two additional ASGW members in the locality of the alleged violation.

d. The charged party(ies) will have not more than 30 days in which to answer the charges in writing. The charged party(ies) will have free access to all cited evidence from which to make a defense, including the right to legal counsel.

e. Based upon the investigation of the Committee and any designated local ASGW members, the following recommendations may be made to the Executive Board for appropriate action:

1. Advise that the charges be dropped
2. Reprimand and admonishment against repetition of the charged conduct
3. Suspension of membership for a specified period from ASGW and/or APGA.
4. Dismissal from membership in ASGW and/or APGA with dismissal made known to ASGW membership through special correspondence.

GUIDELINES FOR TRAINING GROUP LEADERS
Association for Specialists in Group Work

Preamble

Whereas counselors may be able to function effectively with individual clients, they are also required to possess specialized knowledge and skills which render them effective in group work. The Association for Specialists in Group Work support the preparation of group practitioners as part of and in addition to other aspects of counselor education. The Guidelines for Training Group Leaders represent the minimum core of group leader competence which have been identified by the Association for Specialists in Group Work as needed at the cognitive and applied levels.

A. Group Leader Knowledge Competencies:

The group leader has demonstrated specialized knowledge in the following aspects of group work:

A-1. Major theoretical approaches to group work; the distinguishing characteristics of each and the commonalities shared by all.

A-2. The basic principles of group dynamics and the therapeutic ingredients of groups.

A-3. The personal factors of group leaders which have an impact on members; knowledge of personal strengths, weaknesses, biases, values and their impact on others.

A-4. The specific ethical problems unique to group work.

A-5. The body of research on group work.

A-6. The major modes of group work, differentiation among the modes, and the appropriate instances in which each is used.

A-7. The process components of group work.

A-8. The major facilitative and debilitative roles that group members may take.

A-9. The advantages and disadvantages of group work and the circumstances for which it is indicated or contraindicated.

B. Group Leader Skill Competencies:

The group leader has demonstrated the:

B-1. Ability to screen and assess readiness levels of prospective clients.

B-2. Ability to deliver a clear, concise, and complete definition of group counseling.

B-3. Ability to diagnose self-defeating behaviors in group members.

B-4. Ability to describe and operationalize a personally selected group counseling model.

B-5. Ability to appropriately model characteristics of a fully functioning person.

B-6. Ability to accurately interpret non-verbal behavior among group members.

B-7. Ability to exhibit appropriate pacing skills.

B-8. Ability to intervene at critical incidents in the group process.

B-9. Ability to deal with disruptive group members.

B-10. Ability to utilize the major strategies, techniques, and procedures of group counseling.

B-11. Ability to facilitate potent group therapeutic forces.

B-12. Ability to use adjunct group structures such as the use of psychological homework.

B-13. Ability to use basic group leader interventions.

B-14. Ability to stimulate therapeutic conditions by group members.

B-15. Ability to work smoothly and effectively with a co-leader.

B-16. Ability to close sessions and terminate the group process.

TRAINING IN CLINICAL PRACTICE

Number of hours suggested

Supervised Experience	Minimum	Preferred	Ideal
Critique of group tapes	5 hours	15 hours	30 hours
Observer of group counseling	5 hours	15 hours	30 hours
Participant as a client in a group	15 hours	25 hours	50 hours
Coleading a group with a supervisor	15 hours	25 hours	50 hours
Coleading a group with a partner and receiving critical feedback from supervisor	25 hours	40 hours	75 hours

Practicum:

	Minimum	Preferred	Ideal
Leading group along with critical self-analysis of performance; supervisor feedback on tape and self-analysis	25 hours	45 hours	75 hours
Internship: Practice as group leader with supervision "on the job"	25 hours	45 hours	75 hours

Continuing Education and Training:

Evidence of ongoing supervision during first three years of leading groups

Evidence of ongoing training and self-scrutiny throughout professional career

To the owner of this book:

We hope that you have enjoyed the Manual for Theory and Practice of Group Counseling. We'd like to know as much about your experiences with the manual as possible. Only through your comments and the comments of others can we learn how to make the manual a better book for future readers.

School: _____ Your Instructor's Name: _____

1. What I like most about this manual is: _____

_____

_____

2. What I like least about this manual is: _____

_____

_____

3. Specific suggestions for improving the manual are: _____

_____

4. Some ways I used this manual in class were: _____

_____

5. Some ways that I used this manual out of class were: _____

_____

6. Some of the manual's exercises that were used most meaningfully in my

class were: _____

_____

7. My general reaction to this manual is: _____

8. In the space below or in a separate letter, please let us know what other comments about the book you'd like to make. We welcome your suggestions!

_____

_____

_____

Please write down the name of the course in which you used this manual:

_____

Optional:

Your Name: _____ Date: _____

May Brooks/Cole quote you, either in promotion for the Manual for Theory and Practice of Group Counseling or in future publishing ventures?

Yes _____ No _____

Sincerely,

Gerald Corey

FOLD HERE

FOLD HERE

| FIRST CLASS |
| Permit No. 84 |
| Monterey, CA |

BUSINESS REPLY MAIL
No Postage Necessary if Mailed in United States

Dr. Gerald Corey
Brooks/Cole Publishing Company
Monterey, CA 93940